THE ESSENTIALS
OF ECONOMICS

THE
ESSENTIALS OF
ECONOMICS

An Introduction and Outline
for Students and for the
General Reader

BY

DOUGLAS C. HAGUE

Professor in Applied Economics
University of Manchester

AND

ALFRED W. STONIER

Professor of Economic Theory
Makere University College,
Kampala, Uganda

1724

LONGMANS

LONGMANS, GREEN AND CO LTD
48 Grosvenor Street, London W.1
*Associated companies, branches and representatives
throughout the world*

First published 1955
Second impression 1956
Third impression 1963
Fourth impression 1964
Fifth impression 1965

Permission has been given for this book
to be transcribed into Braille

PRINTED IN GREAT BRITAIN
BY R. & R. CLARK, LTD., EDINBURGH

PREFACE

In *A Textbook of Economic Theory* (Longmans, 1953) we attempted to summarise and interpret the techniques and modes of thought which the great economists have used in making their contributions to economic science. The aim of this book is different. It is to explain the main generalisations of present-day economics in simple and straightforward language, using only those few technical terms which are essential for accurate expression.

DOUGLAS HAGUE
ALFRED STONIER

UNIVERSITY COLLEGE, LONDON
October 1954

CONTENTS

INTRODUCTION

MANY questions spring automatically to the mind of anyone who takes an intelligent interest today in current economic affairs. Such questions are : Why did the price of commodities like wool rise so sharply after war broke out in Korea? Why do firms spend so much money on advertising? What difference does it make if the Bank of England alters 'Bank Rate'? Why can we be allowed to spend only a limited amount of money each year on foreign travel? And why does a pound buy a different number of francs, lire or kroner at various times?

In this book we shall not attempt to answer such questions in all their complex detail. The exact importance of the various influences at work will differ from time to time. We shall, however, try to show what are the essential factors on which such problems always depend. This immediately raises the basic difficulty of all economics. The only way in which it is possible to provide a simple outline of the fundamental features and problems of the modern economy is by following the traditional methods of 'deductive' economic analysis. One must use observation and common sense to determine what are the most important facts in any situation which one wishes to explain. One must then proceed from assumptions about these underlying facts to draw generally applicable conclusions. In doing this, however, one can do little more than rely on the assumptions that have become generally accepted by economists. For it is here that the economist meets with a problem that does not often beset the chemist or physicist. In economics it is impossible to carry out a controlled experiment either inside or outside a laboratory.

There are three main reasons for this inability to experiment. First, economists are not in a position to experiment with either individual consumers or individual business-men. In those instances where there is no way of experimenting save with a whole economy, such experiments are even more obviously out of the question. A Chancellor of the Exchequer might be most interested in discovering what would be the effects in Britain of lowering the average weekly wage to £1 or 10s.; but he would never dare to try to discover these effects by actually reducing wages to such levels. Second, even where a particular change in the economy is made by common consent, it is never easy to control other conflicting forces. A truly 'controlled' experiment is impossible. Instead the economic analyst must set to work, and concentrate his attention on the essentials of the problem by assuming 'all other things equal'. Third, any modern economy is so elaborate and complex that it would be quite out of the question for any observer or group of observers, however keen or carefully trained, to trace out all the many results of any given change in that economy.

For these reasons, all useful studies of economic problems must proceed by concentrating attention solely on the salient factors affecting the particular issues. Assumptions are made about the facts of the situation, assumptions which are based on common-sense knowledge of the world, reinforced by more detailed statistical and other evidence, where this is available. For example, as we shall see in Chapter I, economists assume that when the price of a good rises, less of the good is bought. Such generalisations are then explained in terms of individual behaviour. The task of the economist is to discover a pattern of individual behaviour which agrees with common-sense knowledge of the way in which most people act, and the kind of motives which actuate them, seeking confirmation for his views in the findings of psychology and other sciences.

Sometimes the economist approaches his problem from the opposite direction. Starting from assumptions about individual behaviour, the economist reaches general conclusions about the results which such behaviour would produce in the aggregate. For example, in Chapter II we proceed from the assumption that business-men aim at making as much money as possible to show how firms and industries will price their products. These general conclusions about 'aggregates' are then tested, in 'applied economics', by comparing them with statistical and other 'objective' evidence.

CHAPTER I

THE CONSUMER

ECONOMISTS are agreed that one generalisation about the consumer is acceptable to common sense. This is that consumers will normally buy more of a commodity if its price falls and less if its price rises, assuming, of course, that the consumers' money incomes remain constant when the price change occurs. We shall proceed to show that this generalisation about the way in which purchases of a commodity respond to changes in its price can reasonably be explained in terms of a theory of how people behave.

There may perhaps be exceptions to the rule that consumers buy more of a good at a lower price and less at a higher one; but it is agreed by economists that there cannot be many. It is true that a consumer may buy a *constant* amount of some commodities, however high or low their prices are. There will, however, only very occasionally be instances where a consumer actually buys *more* of a good if its prices rises. In all this, of course, we are assuming throughout that the physical constitution of the good in question remains unaltered.

This is the traditional view of economists who have studied the reactions of consumers to changes in prices. The accepted explanation is as follows.[1] When the price of a good changes, the results of that change are said to represent a 'price effect'. This price effect is itself the net result of two subsidiary 'effects'. First, the fall in the price of any given good will mean that it is now cheaper compared with other goods which the consumer previously bought, and whose prices have remained unchanged. He will therefore substitute the cheaper good for those whose prices have remained unchanged, and which are therefore now relatively dearer. This response by the consumer is known as the 'substitution effect'. He substitutes goods which are now relatively cheaper for those which are now relatively dearer.

[1] For a detailed explanation of the currently accepted theory of consumer demand, see *A Textbook of Economic Theory*, A. W. Stonier and D. C. Hague, Longmans, 1953, chapters iii and iv.

The strength of this substitution effect will obviously vary considerably from one good to another. Some goods will have very close substitutes; others will have only very remote ones. For example, if the price of lamb falls, but mutton, pork and beef remain at the same price, the consumer will tend to buy more lamb and less of the other kinds of meat. They are all good substitutes for each other, since they all serve the same kind of purpose. On the other hand, there will be little competition, in the individual consumer's estimation, between bread and underwear. A fall in the price of bread may lead the consumer to 'substitute' bread for other foods; it is not likely to lead him to buy bread instead of underwear. It follows that the strength of the substitution effect will vary, according to whether the goods in question are close, or only distant, substitutes for each other.

The second result of a fall in the price of a good bought by a consumer is known as the 'income effect'. If the price of one of the goods bought by a consumer falls, his 'real' income will rise. In other words, the goods and services which his income will now buy will give him more satisfaction than those he could previously afford. For, out of the same money income, he can buy more of some goods and no less of any others. He is better off in the same kind of way as he would have been if all prices had remained the same but his money income had increased. This is the 'income effect'.

It will be worth our while to look at the income and the substitution effects separately. For the nature of the 'price effect' will obviously depend on the nature of these two component parts of it. Let us first consider the income effect in isolation—the 'pure' income effect.

The essential feature of the income effect, as we have seen, is that it represents that part of the 'price effect' which results solely from the change in the consumer's *real* income. The 'pure' income effect can therefore be seen in a situation where all relative prices are constant (so that there can be no substitution effect resulting from changes in relative prices) but the consumer's *real* income alters. The most convenient way to show this here is to assume that the consumer's *money* income remains constant but *all* prices fall *by the same percentage*. Thus, relative prices will remain constant, but, since all prices have fallen, the consumer's fixed money income will allow him to buy more goods and services—his *real* income will have risen.

The question now is, 'What will be the result of this rise in real income on the consumer's purchases of any given good?' In other words, 'What result will the "income effect" have on purchases of this given good?' With almost every commodity a rise in a consumer's real income will lead him to increase his purchases. Finding that his money will 'go further', the consumer will spend a little more in almost all directions; he will buy a little more of almost all goods. It is true that his purchases of some goods may not alter. Having reached a certain standard of living, the consumer may feel that he has enough of some basic 'necessities' like bread, salt, and even house-room; and he will not purchase any more of these things as his real income rises further. With most goods, however, the consumer will buy more if his real income rises.

The strength of the 'income effect' will therefore vary according to the good in question, just as that of the substitution effect does. However, leaving such peculiarities of individual goods on one side for the moment, the income effect will still vary in strength. It will be strong where the fall in the price of the given good is substantial, and where the consumer previously spent a considerable proportion of his income on that good. It will be weak where the fall in the price of the good concerned is small, and where the consumer spent only a little of his income on that good.

We now consider the 'pure' substitution effect. To do this, we must first eliminate the income effect from the price effect. We can do this quite simply. Let us assume that the price of a given good has fallen and the consumer has adjusted his purchases of it to take account of its lower price. As a result of this 'price effect' the consumer will not only have substituted the cheaper good for those which are now relatively dearer; he will also have adjusted his purchases to take account of his increased real income. This latter 'income effect' can be eliminated if we assume that there is a 'compensating change' in the consumer's real income. A money tax, say, is levied, and is of such a size that it just cancels out, or 'compensates for', the increase in real income that resulted from the fall in the price of the good. We have now isolated the 'pure' substitution effect by eliminating the income effect.

Economists are agreed that this 'pure' substitution effect will *always* mean that the consumer buys more of a cheaper good. In other words, if the price of *only one* of the goods which a consumer buys falls, and that fall is not allowed to alter the consumer's real income, there will be a substitution effect only. This substitution effect will *always* lead the consumer to substitute the good which is now relatively cheaper for all the other goods he buys, and which have become relatively dearer.

We may now return to the 'price effect'. When the price of a good falls, the consumer will buy more of it for two reasons. He will buy more, first, because it is now cheaper than any competing goods, and therefore fulfils the same kind of functions as they do, but somewhat more cheaply. This is the substitution effect. He will buy more, secondly, because now that the given good is cheaper, his given money income will go further. He can buy more of several of the goods he has already been buying, including the good whose price has fallen. This is the income effect. Between them, the income and the substitution effects will make up the price effect; and it follows from what we have already said, that both of them will normally lead the consumer to purchase more of a commodity which becomes cheaper.

Now, in general, one can reasonably suppose that the substitution effect will be the more important in causing the consumer to buy more of a good whose price has fallen. Whilst it is certain that the cheaper good will not be a substitute for *all* the other goods and services that the consumer buys, it is likely to be a fairly good substitute for some of them. But, for a given fall in the price of a particular good, the income effect will only be strong in those, perhaps comparatively rare, cases where the consumer has previously been spending a high percentage of his income on the good in question.

Let us now sum up the argument. The income and substitution effects of a price change will usually reinforce each other, in the sense that both will normally lead the consumer to buy more of a good whose price has fallen. The substitution effect *must* work to increase purchases of the good whose price has fallen; the income effect will normally do the same. Because the fall in the good's price has made him better off, the consumer will want to buy more of this and of most other goods.

The effect of a fall in the price of any good will therefore be to increase consumers' purchases of that good. But one suspects that whilst substitution effects will usually be fairly strong, the income effects may be quite weak. For it is unlikely that consumers will spend a large proportion of their incomes on more than one or two goods, for example, housing and certain types of food. It is, moreover, interesting to note that even with a commodity like bread, where a consumer's expenditure is probably quite considerable, the income effect seems nevertheless to be weak. For bread is always quoted as an instance of a good whose purchases respond little to a fall in price.

We have already noted a limiting case which may be an exception to the general rule set out above, where the consumer does not buy any more of a good at all if it becomes cheaper. Salt is probably a good example of such a commodity. There is no real substitute for salt, so that there is likely to be little or no substitution effect if salt becomes cheaper or dearer. Again, a Briton will normally spend only a very small percentage of his income on salt, so that even a substantial change in its price will cause only a negligible income effect. And even if there *is* an income effect, any rise in real income will normally be expended in buying more of other goods rather than in buying more salt.

It is clear, then, that a consumer's purchases will respond very much more to a change in the prices of some goods than of others. Where the substitution and the income effects are both strong, a fall in the price of a given good will lead the consumer to buy much more of that good. Where the income and substitution effects are both weak there will be little change in purchases. Economists have found it necessary to invent a technical term which enables them to distinguish situations where there is no response in the purchases of a good to a fall in its price; those where there is only a small response; and those where there is a very large increase in purchases if price falls. This technical term is 'elasticity of demand'.

Where a fall in the price of a good leads to no change at all in the amount of the good that is purchased we say that the 'elasticity of demand' for that good is zero. Where a small price reduction leads to an indefinitely large increase in the purchases of a good, we say that the demand for the good is infinitely elastic. In practice, elasticity of demand will nearly always lie between these two limits. The demand for almost all goods will display some elasticity, but never infinite elasticity.

Economists distinguish particularly between those goods with high elasticities of demand and those with low ones. For short, they speak of the difference between goods which have 'elastic' demands and those with 'inelastic' demands.

The demand for a given good is 'elastic' if a small fall in its price causes the total amount of money spent on it to increase,

(Ceteris Paribus relationships are used here)

and a small rise in its price lowers total consumers' expenditure on it. This is true whether one considers expenditure by an individual consumer or by all consumers in a particular market. Similarly, the demand for a good is 'inelastic' if the total expenditure of consumers on that good diminishes when its price is reduced, or increases when its price rises. This is, of course, still assuming that the total *money* incomes of all consumers remain the same both before and after the price change.

It should be noted that, even where the demand for a good is inelastic, the total amount of the good which is bought increases somewhat if the good becomes cheaper. But it increases so slowly as price falls that *total expenditure* on the good diminishes when its price is reduced. Purchases do not rise proportionally to the fall in price. Similarly, when demand is elastic a fall in the price of a good again increases the amount of it that is bought; but there is here a significant difference, namely that the total amount of money spent on the good by consumers rises instead of falling. The amount of the good bought rises *more than in proportion* to the fall in its price.

It will obviously often be extremely important to business-men whether the demand for their product is elastic or inelastic. For example, early in 1954 the London Transport System introduced reduced fares for rail journeys into London after 4.30 P.M. It was explained at the time that the success of the scheme would depend on whether the price reductions encouraged a more than proportionate increase in the number of people travelling. In other words, it was announced that the scheme would fail unless the demand for evening trips to London were elastic, and the lower prices therefore led to an increase in passengers' total expenditure on travel.

On the other hand, of course, if the elasticity of demand for a product is very low, a business-man is likely to increase his profits if he *raises* his price. For a rise in the price of a good with an inelastic demand will increase the total expenditure of consumers on that good. The producer's receipts will rise if he sells a smaller output at a higher price, whilst his total costs of production at that smaller output are likely to be lower. Hence, the increase in price will lead to bigger profits. Similarly, as we shall see in detail later, the total receipts of the Chancellor of the Exchequer will rise if he increases the tax on a good with a very inelastic demand; they are likely to decline if that demand is highly elastic.

It is also possible, in a very broad and general way, to suggest that the demand for 'necessities' will be less elastic than the demand for 'luxuries'. It is clearly not possible to give any precise definition of either a necessity or a luxury; but most people would agree that goods like bread, tea and house-room are necessary to existence, whilst television sets, ice-cream and theatre tickets are not. It is probable that the demand for such 'luxuries' is relatively elastic. They all have numerous fairly close substitutes, of a kind that goods like bread or salt do not. So, whether or not the income effect is small, the substitution effect will normally lead to a substantial increase in the purchases of a 'luxury' when its price falls, so that total expenditure on the good will rise. Here, again, elasticity of demand is a fairly reliable indicator of a significant economic distinction.

The generalisation that consumers, both as individuals and taken as a group, will buy *less* of a good if its price *rises*, and *more* if its price *falls*, has survived the test of time with little difficulty. It should therefore be understood what assumptions underlie this conclusion. The essential assumptions are that each and every consumer's tastes are both consistent and stable. A consumer whose tastes are not consistent even within themselves, whilst he may exist, is surely not typical. Certainly, if he were typical it would be impossible to generalise about his actions. Again, a consumer whose tastes changed frequently and substantially would ruin the efforts of the most able economic theorist to produce a *consistent.* theory of consumer demand. For example, changes in fashion make it difficult for the manufacturer, the shopkeeper and the economist alike to predict and interpret changes in the demand for clothing.

We should, however, make one qualification to the general rule outlined above. It is likely that one type of circumstance in particular will mean that changes in consumers' tastes may depend directly on prices. This makes it desirable to allow for the possibility that consumers may buy more of a good at a high price and less at a low one.

This exception to our general rule depends on expectations about future price changes. If the price of a good rises, this may, in itself, lead consumers to expect further price rises in the future. Consumers will therefore buy more of the good now, despite the fact that its price has risen, in the hope of forestalling any future price rises. Such behaviour is not uncommon. For example, a rise in the price of a security offered on the Stock

B

Exchange will usually lead at least some people to purchase it now in the expectation that its price will rise still further in the future.

Similarly, in Britain, when war began in 1939 and, more especially, in America when war began in Korea, many consumers indulged in a 'buying spree' to lay in stocks of goods which they thought would become progressively dearer as war brought increased demands, reduced supplies and higher prices. Clearly, it is not unusual for expectations of price rises to lead consumers to purchase more of a good whose price has just risen, and is consequently expected to rise further. It does not follow, of course, that expectations will *always* lead to an increase in the purchases of a good whose price has risen. It is quite possible for a rise in the price of a good to be regarded as an indication that prices have now reached an abnormally high 'peak'. So, the expectation will be that in future prices are more likely to fall than to rise. In these circumstances, a rise in price will markedly *reduce* purchases of the dearer good. Everyone will 'hold back' their purchases in anticipation of a coming fall in prices.

In the same way, a fall in price may induce consumers to buy less of a cheapened good and not more, if it is felt that the current fall in price is a precursor of yet further falls. Consumers will 'hold off' their purchases until they are sure that no more price reductions are in the offing. Conversely, if the result of a price fall is to make people feel that prices have reached 'rock bottom', and are therefore likely to rise sooner or later, the result will be the opposite.

Our explanation of the behaviour of individual consumers has not taken account of the possibility that sometimes a consumer's tastes may themselves be changed by the purchases of other members of society. For example, the desire 'to keep up with the Joneses', or to show off one's own wealth in an effort to gain social prestige, may mean that the consumers' tastes are, in part, determined socially and not individually. It is, however, most unlikely that such social factors will cause any significant exceptions to the general rules that we have outlined above.

CHAPTER II

THE FIRM

LIKE the rest of us, the consumers whose actions were studied in Chapter I had no control over the prices of the goods they bought. Individual consumers can rarely influence the prices they pay. These are said to be set for them by 'the market', or by those never-failing allies of leader-writers and politicians, the 'laws of supply and demand'. In this and the following two chapters we shall discover how the prices of goods are determined.

Using the normal methods of economic analysis, we begin by setting out the assumptions from which our conclusions will be drawn. The time-honoured assumption, which has been used by almost all economists who have contributed to the Theory of the Firm, is that business-men try to earn the largest possible profits—that they attempt to 'maximise' their money profits. It is, of course, obvious that business-men are in business primarily to make money. Indeed, as a first approximation to the truth we may assume that business-men do want to 'maximise' their profits. But whilst this idea that business-men always try to earn the largest possible profits might appear to some people, for example ardent Marxists, as telling the whole story, it clearly does not. It is a very useful first approximation to the truth; but it can rarely, if ever, represent the whole truth. For various reasons, firms will either not wish, or not be able, continually to extort the last pennyworth of profit from their customers. There are five main types of qualification to the business-man's ability to earn the maximum possible profit. Some of these qualifications will mean that even when the business-man's greed is boundless, he is unable to earn maximum profits. Other factors directly limit that greed. For instance, the first qualification to the assumption of profit maximisation depends on the psychology of individual business-men and boards of directors. Some business-men are more interested in the products they make than in the profits they earn. Others are more attracted by the power which running a business gives them over their fellow men than in making a fortune. Yet others may, through laziness or lack of interest, fail to keep costs down to the level one could reasonably expect from men of their ability. However, where competition is keen such factors are inevitably of minor importance; no firm can afford for long to neglect opportunities for earning larger profits by efficient and progressive management.

For short periods, if they have a monopoly of their particular product, or if, perhaps because of general inflation in the economy, conditions are unusually prosperous, firms can ignore the need to devote their main efforts to making profits. In the long run, however, they will find that unless they do produce economically, they will be sent out of business by the competition of more efficient, energetic, and perhaps new, firms.

Second, there are many institutional restraints which prevent firms from continually seeking the absolute maximum of profit. For example, apart from the fact that business-men will themselves be physically incapable of spending more than a certain number of hours at work during any given period of time, workers will normally be willing to work only for a given number of hours each week, that number depending on existing conditions in the society. Nor will they work on, say, Bank Holidays. Similarly, firms will rarely be able to ignore the institutional framework set up by trade unions, employers' organisations and the Government when deciding on their prices and output. For example, double-shift working may be economically desirable but politically and socially unacceptable.

Above all, the growth of the joint-stock company has led to considerable objections to the assumption that firms are only interested in earning the largest possible profit. The fact that the different members of a board of directors can hold different views about the best policy to pursue means that an analysis intended to apply to a one-man firm cannot be used—unless one assumes the latter firm's owner to be suffering from schizophrenia. Again, the managers who run a business will rarely receive much of the profits which they earn, so that the direct connection between an individual's actions and his earnings will usually be very small.

Third, it may not be possible to make the relatively small changes in output that are needed to maximise profits. In some cases only discontinuous changes in the size of the firm may be possible. For instance, the only technically feasible increase in output may be much larger than the market seems to justify.

Again, it may be possible to increase output sufficiently to earn maximum profits only if a completely new factory is built; and this may take time. In the short run the solution would be to try to expand output in the firm's existing plant by persuading workers to work harder or longer. But, whilst it will usually be quite easy to increase output in this way for short periods of time, difficulties may occur if an attempt is made to maintain the increased pace of working for many weeks. For example, it may lead to strikes or to increased absenteeism. It is therefore likely that a sustained increase in output can only come from a physical expansion in the size of the plant. This will take time, so that short-period profit maximisation may be impossible. It follows that the desire of the business-man to make money will be sometimes thwarted by the fact that he can only expand output discontinuously and after the necessary lapse of time.

A fourth reason why the assumption of profit maximisation needs qualification is that business-men are inevitably somewhat ignorant about demand conditions, and especially about the way in which these conditions will change in the future. If business-men knew exactly how much of their product they would be able to sell at all possible prices and over long periods of time they would be able to approach much nearer to maximum profits. In the world as it is, uncertainty and ignorance hold them back. It is only the far-sighted or the lucky who can make large profits in the world as we know it.

The fifth, and final, qualification to profit maximisation is perhaps the most important. It is that whilst business-men will often be interested in making the largest possible *long-term* profits, this may not be consistent with trying at all times to make the largest possible short-run gains. This clash between long-run and short-run profit maximisation will not always occur. A single firm in the world market for, say, cotton will find that long- and short-period profit maximisation come to the same thing. Prices at any moment will be set by 'the market', and no customers will be alienated if at all times the 'world price' is charged. The impersonal forces of the market prevail over any personal feelings. Similarly, in the fashion trades, producers will charge as much as they can for a product before the fashion changes.

There will, however, be many industries where it is more profitable to be content with consistent and modest profits over a long period of time, building up a thriving and expanding business, rather than to make as much as possible in the short run and gain the reputation of exploiting customers. In this type of situation, which is perhaps typical of modern manufacturing industry, one may perhaps make the distinction, suggested by Professor J. R. Hicks, between the 'sticker' and tne 'snatcher'. The 'snatcher' will be the man who is out for large short-term returns, perhaps in order to sell his business at a large profit in the near future. The 'sticker' is concerned with building up a strong, reputable, and in the long run very lucrative, business on the principle of earning moderate profits over many years.

The assumption of profit maximisation, suitably qualified, remains the basic assumption of all economic analysis of the price policies of firms. Further assumptions are necessary, however, especially about the nature of the cost and demand conditions facing the individual firm. Let us first consider its costs.

The costs of any firm can be divided into two types. First, there are the direct (or variable) costs, all those costs whose total amount alters as output changes; these are items like wages and raw material costs. Such charges usually tend to vary in rough proportion to output, so long as output does not exceed the 'normal' capacity of the firm. Consequently, direct costs *per unit of output* remain roughly constant. Once output does exceed this 'normal' level, costs rise sharply. For the firm's plant was not designed to operate efficiently at so high a level of production. As a result, managers and foremen alike will find it difficult to keep production running smoothly. Labour costs may well rise more rapidly than output.

For example, in the cotton industry a weaving shed may be operating efficiently with, say, ten looms per weaver. To meet exceptionally heavy demands this number might be reduced to six or even four. Output would rise somewhat because the weaver would have more time to pay attention to an individual loom; each loom would consequently spend less time standing idle, waiting for attention, when stoppages occurred. But the wage bill would rise more rapidly than output, so that labour costs per unit of output would rise. The same is true of all other direct costs. Thus, once output exceeds the normal capacity of any firm, its direct costs per unit of output will always rise quite sharply. The firm's equipment is being worked too intensively, and 'diminishing returns' consequently begin to set in.

The remainder of the costs of the firm are its overhead (or fixed) costs. 'Overheads' are all those costs which do not vary at all as output changes. They include, for example, rent, rates, charges for depreciation of plant and buildings, insurance premiums, debenture interest, and so on. That part of 'depreciation' which is due to actual 'wear and tear', and not to obsolescence and the passage of time, will, of course, be part of variable, not fixed, costs. The amount of 'wear and tear' will vary with changes in output. So long as a firm remains solvent it must cover all overhead costs, with the result that the *total amount* of these costs remains constant whatever the firm's output. Overhead cost per unit of output therefore declines steadily as the firm's output rises until, by the time the normal capacity output is reached, overheads per unit of output will usually have become quite small. The constant total amount of overhead costs is spread over a progressively larger number of units of output when production rises, and overhead cost per unit of output consequently falls.

The total costs of the firm will be made up of these two categories—direct and overhead costs. It follows that at first the cost per unit of the firm's output will fall fairly rapidly as that output rises from zero towards the capacity level. Direct costs per unit will remain constant, but overhead cost per unit will fall. Over a range of output at and a little below the capacity level, unit costs will remain fairly constant or, more likely, fall rather slowly. The fall in overhead cost per unit will, however, have here become much less rapid and direct costs per unit will be fairly stable, declining only slightly. But when the normal capacity output of the firm is exceeded, unit costs will rise sharply. The fall in overhead cost per unit will by this time have become negligible ; at the same time, direct costs will have begun to rise quite steeply as output increases. Not least among the factors leading to a rise in direct costs will be the increased cost of making sales as larger outputs are produced.

This behaviour of unit costs, falling to begin with and rising later, depends on what are known as the internal economies and diseconomies of production. Unit costs fall over the range of output between zero and normal capacity because rising output enables 'internal economies' of production to be reaped. The firm's internal organisation is such that it can produce with a rather lower unit cost when output is at or near the 'normal capacity' output than when it is small. For example, as output rises the firm can benefit from increased division of labour, each man specialising on one job, with consequent savings in time and effort, and increases in the skill and dexterity of individual workers. Similarly, machinery and other capital equipment is used more fully, and thus more efficiently, at larger outputs, as also are the administrative and sales staffs. For all these reasons, a plant designed to produce a given normal capacity output will produce at a progressively lower unit cost as output rises from zero towards that normal capacity level.

In just the same way, when output exceeds the normal capacity level 'internal diseconomies' of production arise. Capital assets are now worked too fully; management problems arise in organising the unusually large output efficiently; and the energy of workers and of the administrative staff is overtaxed. So, if the normal capacity output of any firm is exceeded, internal diseconomies of production raise unit costs.

To sum up, internal economies at levels of output below normal capacity, and internal diseconomies at or beyond that capacity output, account for the fact that any firm's unit costs will fall to begin with and will tend to rise when its normal capacity output is exceeded.

The demand conditions facing the firm will depend essentially on whether it is producing under competition or monopoly. Where the firm has many competitors, all producing the same or similar products, the price at which its output can be sold will be determined within very narrow limits by the prices of these competing goods. Where the firm has no close competitors, its owner will have greater latitude in fixing his own price. However competitive or monopolistic conditions are, the fundamental fact will always be that the firm can sell more of a given product at a lower price, and less at a higher one. When the firm has a monopoly of its product, the demand for that product is not likely to be very elastic. A reduction in price may not lead to any significant increase in sales; it may, indeed, cause a fall in the firm's total receipts, because demand is actually inelastic. On the other hand, where there is keen competition the demand for the firm's product will be elastic so that a small price reduction will also increase the firm's total receipts.

The business-man must, however, not only keep himself informed about the changes in his sales which would occur if, at a given moment, he were to lower his price. He must also consider whether, at a given price, his sales are likely to rise or fall over the foreseeable future. For, if he feels that future demand is likely to be buoyant, he may be able to earn profits by expanding his productive capacity in advance of these improving demand conditions.

On the basis of the above assumptions, we may outline the way in which business-men fix the price and output of their product. First, a word of warning. One often gets the impression, in discussing this subject with business-men, that they fix their prices and their output separately. As we have just seen, this is not possible. At any given price, the amount of a firm's product which consumers will take depends quite closely on that price. Similarly, if a firm decides how big an output it will produce, the price which it will have to charge in order just to dispose of that output is automatically determined. Despite any illusions, the business-man will have constantly to consider both his price and his output as he makes his decisions.

At any given moment, each firm will have a plant with a given capacity output. The ideal solution will therefore be one where the business-man can fix a price which not only seems to enable him to earn maximum profits, but which also enables him to do so by producing at, or very near to, his normal capacity. In such circumstances his pricing decision will be relatively straightforward. The business-man will begin by calculating the cost of producing each unit of output at this capacity level; to this unit cost he will add what he considers to be the most satisfactory profit margin. In general, the main factors determining the size of this profit margin will be the degree of competition facing the firm, and the nature of demand conditions. After allowing for the type of qualification to the principle of profit maximisation outlined above, the size of the profit margin will depend essentially on these two factors. Where there are many competing firms in the industry and/or rather depressed demand conditions the profit margin will be small. Where there are few rivals and/or very buoyant demand conditions, profit margins will be bigger.

Another vital factor determining the size of profit margins is whether or not the firm is able and willing to take advantage of opportunities to reap considerable temporary profits, or whether it is more interested in long-term profits. As we have seen, a firm making fashion articles knows that the market for any particular article will not last for very long. It will therefore 'make what it can whilst the going is good' by charging a fairly high price for the short period of time when the article in question is 'in vogue'. On the other hand, we have also noticed that where an article is expected to represent a 'bread and butter line' for many years, the firm selling it will usually avoid the temptation to charge high prices in the early stages. Profits from selling the article will not be maximised by charging high prices over short periods when conditions are good, and perhaps thereby alienating customers. Small margins and steady sales over a long period will be the best way to earn large profits. It follows that the basic principle of profit maximisation can lead to many and varied price-output policies in practice.

Similarly, there will be no absolute uniformity in the reactions of the individual firm if the demand for its product increases at a time when it is already producing its normal capacity output. For instance, if a firm has no serious competitors, it may allow its order book to lengthen for some time, rather than try to push output even higher. Other firms, on the other hand, especially those with many rivals, will do all that they can to expand output in the short run, by working overtime or by working two or three shifts. In the long run, however, all firms will tend to expand their capacity when demand has risen. Whether this kind of buoyant demand will call forth higher prices will depend on the circumstances. If the firm has many rivals, competitive pressure is likely to raise prices when the first increase in demand occurs, though prices will drop again when the long-term expansion in the various firms' capacity has taken place.

If the firm has few rivals, however, it may decide not to alter prices at all until some time has elapsed. For one thing, there will be purely administrative objections to price changes in those firms where detailed price-lists are published. Thus, whilst a greengrocer or a barrow-boy will change his prices from day to day, even from hour to hour, prices for clothing will normally be fixed 'for the season'; those of other goods with published price-lists will only be altered at infrequent intervals. Again, prices on world markets, for goods like wheat and tin, as well as prices of stock exchange securities and foreign currencies will alter almost from minute to minute throughout the day. There is, once again, no uniform pattern for the behaviour of prices, they will change differently in different firms and industries.

Similar differences will occur if the demand for any firm's product falls off. If output is reduced, overhead costs per unit of output will rise, the total (fixed) amount of overheads being spread over a smaller number of articles. To cover unit costs, it might therefore appear necessary to *raise* prices. This is not likely to happen, however. Firms will decide either to sell their goods for what they will fetch—even if this means running at a loss for some time ; or they will decide to close down temporarily to avoid 'spoiling the market', if only by giving workers an extra fortnight's summer holiday. Only in exceptional circumstances can profits be maintained by *raising* prices during a slump.

The only real conclusion that can be reached on the nature of the firm's price-output policy, then, is that it will differ according to circumstances. Fortunately, however, we shall be able as we proceed to show what the most likely circumstances are, and how the individual firm will frame its policy to suit them.

We have, so far, regarded the location of all firms as given. In practice, however, a business-man setting up a new factory will decide where to build it in the light of the same general principles as those on which he bases his price policy. Ideally, he should calculate what costs he would incur in all the possible sites available to him. He would, for example, work out how much it would cost, at each possible site, to transport raw materials to the factory and to distribute its product ; he would calculate the cost of rent, rates, heat, light and power in the various sites. Similarly, he would calculate the cost of hiring, and if necessary training, workers, foremen and managers in the various potential sites, and similarly for all other items of cost. From these cost estimates, and from estimates of the markets available to him, either nationally or locally, the business-man would be able to discover which of all the various locations available to him would offer him the highest profits. Once again the desire for maximum profits would be likely to determine his choice.

In practice, the decision will not be quite so simple or straight-forward. A business-man is usually able to make his decision only within a relatively limited horizon. For example, the man setting up a small shop may know little about conditions outside his own town. He will therefore ignore sites outside it. Again, a firm may refrain from setting up its factory on what appears to be the most profitable site because it does not want to cut itself off from the intangible and immeasurable benefits often to be gained from setting up production in a traditional centre of the industry. On the other hand, of course, the business-man may sometimes deliberately avoid the traditional centres of the trade because the conservatism of workers or managers makes it impossible to use the most modern methods of production or, for example, work three shifts a day, unless one sets up production well away from that traditional centre with all the advantages it offers.

Finally, the business-man may not be allowed to choose freely. The Government may direct that, for strategic reasons, certain firms must be set up in remote parts of the country. Again, if some areas of the country are severely depressed, with much unemployment, firms may be compelled by law, or induced by the offer of low rents, or outright money subsidies, to move away from the more prosperous regions to these 'depressed' areas.

To conclude this chapter we touch on a different, but related, point. One has merely to look at the world around one to notice that there are strong factors limiting the size of the individual firm. Firms do not often grow to be as large as the miracles of modern technology might lead one to anticipate. This question has naturally interested economists, and they have drawn attention to two important factors which, separately or together, seem to limit the size of firms. First, there is the fact that as a firm becomes larger a point is inevitably reached where unit costs, both of production and of making sales, rise sharply. Second, there is the likelihood that the demand for any firm's product will not be unlimited, and that to sell very large amounts of its produce the price charged would have to be very low indeed.

It seems likely that rising costs of the kind just mentioned are more important in limiting the size of firms in industries where there is keen competition. In monopoly, it is the limited size of the market which is the dominant factor. In a competitive industry, the individual firm is so small that it can take the ruling 'competitive' price as given. Hence, it could easily expand its sales considerably, if only it could profitably cut its price somewhat, and thus gain trade at the expense of rivals. The fact that individual firms do remain quite small in competitive industries like, say, farming and clothing manufacture, implies that such price cutting cannot there be successfully carried out. In other words, once the output of such competitive firms exceeds a certain, moderate level, costs rise sharply; and it is impossible for the firm profitably to expand in size—except at a level of prices considerably above the existing competitive level. It is impossible to undercut the other firms in the industry and continue to make money.

In the case of monopolies, however, the evidence of economists suggests that firms often fail to expand where they could produce a larger output at a lower cost per unit. It is here the limited size of the market which ensures that, whilst increased output could be produced at lower costs, it could only be sold at give-away prices. It is the size of the market which is the factor preventing an increase in the size of the large, monopolistic firm. A direct result of the size of the market is that the firm's knowledge of the nature of that market is limited. Market research may enable a firm to discover a bigger field for its goods. Consequently, the growth of the large firm depends largely on whether its market research and sales staffs can enable it to take advantage of the lower costs which larger production could give. It is not far from the truth to say that the growth of large firms depends on a perpetual struggle by its sales staff to keep up with the production possibilities provided by its technicians.

CHAPTER III

COMPETITION

COMPETITION occurs where a large number of firms makes similar products, and it has long attracted the attention of economists. In some cases all the firms in a competitive industry will produce identical, or 'homogeneous' products. For example, wheat is wheat, whoever grows it, and all the world's many producers of wheat receive the same 'competitive' price.

With most industrial products, however, the situation is rather different. The clothing industry, for example, is made up of a large number of firms producing very similar products. But these products are certainly not identical, and the prices of, say, raincoats, will differ greatly between firms. Nevertheless, keen competition between the various producers will prevent such price differences becoming excessive. Each producer, even in such a competitive industry, has the 'monopoly' of his own individual product, by virtue, perhaps, of a trade name or trademark. But all these various products compete keenly in the industry's general market.

In such a situation, the various products will not differ significantly from each other; each product will be slightly *differentiated* from the others. Every producer will attempt to convince consumers that, although his own product serves fundamentally the same purpose as all the others, it has that 'extra something' which they have not. In these circumstances, we say that there is 'product differentiation'.

Let us now consider how a competitive industry will determine its selling price and its output. We first discuss the simplest type of situation, where all products are identical and, since there are many firms in the industry, competition is keen. Such a situation is met with in many agricultural markets and in markets for some intermediate industrial products like given qualities of wool 'tops' or cotton yarn and fabric. Since all firms' products are identical, and since any individual producer is responsible only for an extremely small proportion of the total output of the industry, he must take the existing 'market' price as given and need only adjust his output so as to earn what he considers the most satisfactory amount of profit. The elasticity of demand for the firm's product is infinite; a small reduction in price would increase the *individual firm's* sales indefinitely, and at the existing price it can sell as much as it will ever wish to sell.

We have already seen that business men will rarely attempt to earn the absolute maximum of profit; instead they will try to maximise these profits subject to the constraints inherent in their own psychology and the institutions of contemporary society. Nevertheless, in a keenly competitive industry, there will be relatively little room for manœuvre. Once the firm has realised the necessity for accepting the constraints imposed on all firms by the existing social structure, it is, to put the point somewhat crudely, almost a case of 'maximise or go bust'. The 'margins of tolerance' within which each firm in a competitive industry has to work will be very small.

To see in detail how demand and supply between them determine the price of the product for the whole industry, let us consider an industry in which the price and output of the product in question have both been roughly constant at the existing level for some time, subject only to small and short-lived fluctuations. It follows that the amount of the product which the industry is supplying is sufficient, and only just sufficient, to meet the existing demand at the existing price. Otherwise that price would alter. It does not follow, however, either that all firms are making profits, or that there is no movement of firms into or out of the industry.

In any such position, where the total output of the whole competitive industry is fairly stable, some firms will be losing money, some earning large profits and some just covering their costs. Some of the firms which are losing money may be those which have recently entered the industry and have yet to make their position in it secure; others may even fail to survive this initial period of consolidation; yet others will be old firms which are on the way out of the industry after a long and prosperous life. Now complete freedom of entry into the industry is a *sine qua non* of keen competition. Any restrictions on entry will conflict with the fundamental prerequisite that the number of firms in the industry must be, and must remain, large. Thus, the essential condition which has to be satisfied, if price and output in such a competitive industry are to remain stable, is that the rate at which firms are entering the industry must be such as exactly to cancel out the loss of output from firms which are leaving it.

This condition, in turn, will depend for its fulfilment on the general level of profits in the industry. If profits are high, many new firms will be lured into the industry by the prospect of high returns; if the general level of profits is low, many of the less efficient firms in the industry will lose money and more firms than usual will be forced to leave it. In order to keep the total output of the industry constant, the general level of profits must be such as neither to attract an abnormally large number of new firms nor to drive out an abnormally large number of existing ones. Such a general rate of profits will occur when the number of firms making high profits, the number sustaining losses and the number just covering their costs are such as business-men wondering whether to enter the industry would 'normally' expect to find. In economic jargon, we say that the industry is then earning 'normal' profits.

The foregoing analysis does, of course, depend on the notion that there is a typical 'life cycle' for the individual firm. The firm will begin its life relatively small and weak and will lose money fairly consistently during an initial 'growing period'. From then on, the firm will make money consistently, rising towards its zenith as its owner increases in maturity and experience. Finally, it will decline as increasing age, conservatism and technical backwardness take their toll. This kind of notion is clearly reasonable in the kind of industry we are at present considering—one where there is a large number of relatively small firms. Where such a firm is run by an individual owner, it is inevitable that its efficiency will be largely a function of his age. Even where the firm is a limited liability company, however, a similar 'life cycle' is likely to occur, though it may cover a longer period of time, and there may be numerous fluctuations in efficiency and profitability.

Let us now consider what will happen if the demand for the industry's product alters. First, what happens if there is a large and permanent increase in the demand for the product so that, at any price, consumers would buy considerably more of the product than at present? In order to answer this question fully, we must make an important distinction—between the long period and the short period. The short period we may define, following the great Alfred Marshall, as that period of time during which extra production can only be obtained if the existing plants in the industry use their existing capital equipment more fully, by increasing the number of workers employed. In the long period such restraints disappear. We define the long period as a period of time long enough for existing firms to alter the amount of their capital equipment, for new firms to be set up and for extra skilled workers to be trained. Because of this fundamental difference in the way in which production conditions will respond, when sufficient time has elapsed, the short-period effects of a substantial increase in demand will differ from those in the long period.

The short-period price of any product is bound to rise substantially in the face of a large increase in demand. To begin with, it is true, the increased demand may be met by drawing on existing stocks. If these are large, they may 'cushion' any price rise for some time. But they cannot adequately deal with a large and sustained rise in demand of the kind we are studying.

The initial result of an increased demand for a good is therefore a sharp price rise of the kind experienced in the wool, tin and other commodity markets immediately after the outbreak of the Korean war. At the existing price, the amount demanded considerably exceeds the amount supplied and the price rises substantially. Rather than go away empty-handed, buyers are prepared to bid up prices against each other, and, from their relatively small stocks, producers will not be able significantly to increase supplies to take immediate advantage of the higher prices. It is worth noting that in this type of market there is no reluctance on the part of sellers to raise prices. Since the product is homogeneous and the firms are small, 'goodwill' is unimportant. The 'impersonal forces of the market' prevail over the personal feelings of individual producers and there is no hesitation in raising prices. As a result, all producers experience exactly the same price increase; all raise their prices equally.

Once the initial impact of the changed demand conditions has had this effect on market prices, the more permanent short-period result of higher prices is to increase both output and profits. The higher price makes it profitable to incur the increased costs met with when output is pushed beyond the 'normal' capacity level. Nor, when competition is keen, can firms respond to prosperity in the industry by allowing order books to lengthen, instead of attempting to earn maximum profits through expanding

C

output beyond the normal limits. For their rivals will be only too ready to compete for the custom of those who are experiencing delivery delays—at slightly higher prices.

The industry's short-period increase in output will, however, be relatively small and hard-won. Since it takes some time to expand the capacity of any firm, the short-run method of increasing output is to work the existing plant more intensively, pushing output beyond the 'normal' capacity level. This means greater strain on the capital equipment and, more especially, on human beings. Overtime rates will probably have to be paid, skilled labour may be short and wages may rise. Above all, in attempting to use the existing capital equipment more intensively, the proportion of labour to capital will increase and, quite apart from any danger of rising wage rates, the 'law of diminishing returns' will operate. Quite simply, this 'law' states that if additional men are working with given capital equipment, as happens in expanding the short-run output of a firm, then, after a certain point, the output obtained will rise less than in proportion to the increase in the number of men employed. 'Returns' will diminish, and costs will rise. For all these reasons, the short-run costs of firms, and therefore prices, will rise sharply if demand increases. Profits will rise too. But whilst this rise in profits may prevent declining firms from leaving the industry at the 'normal' rate, it will be unlikely to alter the rate of entry significantly in the short period. Not until enough time has elapsed for new entrants to build themselves factories will firms begin to enter the industry in sufficient numbers to compete away the high profits being earned.

The long-period results will be quite different. First, firms already in the industry will extend their plants. Rather than work the existing plants so intensively, with output exceeding their 'normal' capacity, they will expand that capacity itself, thereby reducing both the intensity of operations and the strain on workers and management. Firms will increase their 'scale of operations'. Second, increased profits will, in the long run, affect the rate of entry of firms into the industry. More firms than usual will be set up, attracted into the industry by the hope of large gains; similarly, the number of firms going bankrupt will be smaller than usual. For these two reasons everything about the industry will grow. There will be more firms in the industry, and the general size of firms will also increase.

We must now consider the long-run effect of increased demand on prices and output. Output will increase more than in the short run. The increased rate of entry into the industry, coupled with the smaller number of firms being forced out, will result in a net increase both in the industry's output and in the number of firms in the industry. The long-run effects on the price of the industry's product are, however, less certain and will depend on the behaviour of costs. Internal economies and diseconomies of production will still arise in each individual firm at any given scale of operations. In the long run, however, individual firms will expand their capacity. 'Normal capacity' output will be greater than in the short run. But there is no reason to suppose that any further internal economies will result from the increase in the scale of operations of the individual firms themselves. Any reduction in cost which was to be obtained by increasing the scale of the firm's operations could have been obtained in the original equilibrium situation, before the short-run price had risen ; and competition between firms will have ensured that such benefits have already been obtained. Unless new technical developments make more efficient production processes possible, no increase in the scale of operations in the individual firm can lower its costs ; and for the present we shall ignore such technical progress. So far as the individual firm's internal position is concerned, then, long-period costs are unlikely to be lower than in the initial position before demand increased—and they may well be higher.

This does not, of course, mean that any given change in output is as expensive to obtain in the long run as it is in the short run. For in the long period fewer of the firm's costs are fixed and more are variable. To reduce its long-run output, a firm can let part of its premises, or sell them. It can reduce the amount of its capital equipment, and thereby reduce the 'overhead' cost of depreciation. Similarly, increased output can be obtained by setting up a larger plant, specifically designed to produce at this larger output. In the long run, a firm can adapt the scale of its operations to produce any given output as effectively as possible. Even so, it is likely that after a certain level of output is reached, where long-period costs have reached a minimum, any further increase in the firm's 'scale of operations' will raise unit costs. Although a long-run increase in output of the kind we are studying can be obtained at a lower unit cost than can an increase of output in the short run, unit costs will still be somewhat higher than in the original position. For even if there are no technical limits to the economic size of the firm, the task of management will become more difficult once a given size is passed, and costs will therefore rise because production is being organised and controlled less effectively.

If there were no other factors to be considered, then, the general level of long-run costs in a competitive industry would certainly not be lower than before demand increased. Once time has elapsed, therefore, the industry will reach a new position, corresponding to the increased demand, where price and output will again be roughly constant. The total demand and total supply of the industry's product will again be equal—save for minor and short-lived fluctuations. Similarly, the level of profits —and hence the rate of entry to and exit from the industry—will be that which is 'normal' to the new situation. Thus, if the internal economies and diseconomies of production in the individual firms were the only factors to be considered, the fact that the general level of costs will be certainly no lower than originally would ensure that long-period prices were not lower either.

But there are other factors. The main ones are known as *external economies and diseconomies of production* and they result from the change in the scale of operations of the industry as a whole, as distinct from the changes 'internal' to the individual firm which have been studied earlier. One important 'external diseconomy' is almost certain to occur as the output of an industry rises, in response to an increase of demand such as we are studying. As we have seen, new firms will need to be attracted into the industry. But it is almost certain that the managements of such firms will be less skilled and efficient than those already in the industry. The supply of efficient business men to an industry is not inexhaustible, so that the increased output will call for a higher level of profits than was 'normal' before demand rose. Prices (and profits) must increase sufficiently to overcome the 'external diseconomy' of attracting to and maintaining in the industry business men who are less capable than those who were in it to begin with. Similarly, an increase in the output of an industry may raise the prices of its raw materials, if they are not in abundant supply; it may raise wages, and so on. The likelihood of such external diseconomies, taken in conjunction with what has already been said about internal economies and diseconomies, means that, although the long-period price will certainly be below the high short-period price which ruled when profits were abnormally high but there was no flow of new entrants into the industry, it may well be higher than in the initial situation.

This, however, is not quite the whole story. For although the price cannot fall because of internal economies of production, there may be *external* economies. For example, an increase in the size of the whole industry may enable all firms in it to obtain some commodities or services more cheaply. The stock textbook illustration points out that, in a coal-mining area an increase in the size of the industry, bringing more mines, may reduce the cost of pumping water from any one of them. Similarly, a larger industry may be able to organise information services, technical education or improved transport facilities, and thus lower costs in all firms. If such external economies are large enough, they may cancel out, or more than cancel out, increases in other costs. The long-period price may therefore fail to rise; it may even fall.

It is, however, unlikely that such external economies will often enable a competitive industry to expand its output without a rise in costs and prices. Their very nature means that they are almost certain to be of minor importance compared with the various forces leading to increased costs. The main hope of producing an increased output at lower prices must lie in the possibility that technical progress can improve methods of production. Orthodox Anglo-Saxon economics has always ignored this factor, although it is clearly one that should not be overlooked in a complete analysis. Unfortunately technical advances cannot be closely related to underlying economic conditions. There is, for example, no particular reason to suppose that technical advance is necessarily more rapid when an industry is prosperous than when it is depressed; when it is monopolistic than when it is competitive, and so on.

We may now sum up this discussion of the effects of increased demand on a competitive industry. In the initial equilibrium position the price and output of the industry were constant, apart from minor fluctuations. Profits were normal, and the rates of entry to and exit from the industry consequently such as to keep prices stable. Though there were considerable differences in costs and profits between the least and the most efficient firms in the industry, competition was keen and entrepreneurs found it essential to keep a close watch on the efficiency and profitability of their firms.

The short-run results of increased demand were to raise greatly both the price of the industry's product and the level of profits. In the long run these conditions of prosperity increased both the number and the average size of firms. Output rose somewhat above its short-period volume; and price, which had been high in the short run, fell towards the original level. In this new long-period position the industry's price and output were again stable, with normal profits and normal rates of entry and exit. Competition was still keen enough to give business-men little respite in the quest for technical and economic effi-ciency. 'A quiet life' might be attractive; but in such conditions it would hardly be possible.

A similar series of events follows a large once-for-all reduction in the demand for the product of a keenly competitive industry. Supply will now exceed demand and, to begin with, firms will attempt to hold prices up by allowing stocks to rise. This be-haviour will persist only so long as firms can afford to go on increasing their investment in stocks, and are sufficiently opti-mistic to hope that such stocks can be profitably disposed of in the not-too-distant future. When it becomes clear that the falling-off in demand is permanent, prices will fall, perhaps seriously, as stocks are disposed of. Producers will undercut each other; for, since each producer's output is very small compared with that of the whole market, he has no incentive to avoid 'spoiling the market'. Other firms are bound to 'spoil it' even if he does not.

The more permanent short-period result of the fall in demand will therefore be to lower *prices* substantially; but output may not fall very much. One of the most important features of this type of situation is that it will not necessarily be foolish for the firm to sell output below its full unit cost. As we have seen, some of the costs of the firm will be overhead costs, and these will have to be met whether the firm produces any output or not. Consequently, it will often pay firms to go on producing so long as they can cover variable costs and also earn something towards overheads. Firms will still find it profitable to go on producing output so long as the price they receive does not fall below *variable* costs per unit of output. Such 'weak selling', as it is called, will continue for some time, in the face of the kind of permanent and large-scale reduction of demand that we are considering. The main result will be that the capital assets of firms will be run down by their failure to charge a sufficient amount to depreciation.

This very keen 'cut throat' competition will drive profits far below the 'normal' level and the entry of firms into the industry will probably stop. The rate of exit will also be high, partly because entrepreneurs will leave the industry in search of normal profits (or even a steady wage as an employee) elsewhere, and partly because, as we have seen, low prices will mean that some firms are unable to replace plant and machinery. In the long run, therefore, the number of firms in the industry will decline. Price will return to something like the pre-depression level, as will profits.

We can now approach the more practically important problem of how prices are determined in an industry with a large number of firms producing differentiated products, and not the identical products that we have considered so far. In essence the situation is similar; but there are some interesting and significant differences. To begin with, the clear-cut distinction between the keenly competitive situation within the industry and the weaker competition from firms outside it now disappears. Firms producing differentiated products may meet less keen competition from firms within their own industry than from firms outside. Motorcar producers, for example, meet competition, in their attempt to attract consumers' limited incomes, from house-builders, foreign holidays and so on. Television-set manufacturers meet competition from cinemas and theatres as well as from other radio firms. In practice, however, it is usually possible to pick out a group of firms, for example clothing firms, which compete much more keenly with each other than with firms in other industries. It is with such a competitive industry that we are concerned here.

Competition between the many firms in the same industry will be keen. On the one hand, all the products will be of a similar nature and will fulfil similar purposes; on the other hand, these products will be produced by similar processes. Thus, the fact that each firm produces its own individual product, and has its own clientele and its own particular or 'special' market, will give the firm a certain measure of control over the price it charges, the output it produces and the profits it earns. But no such firm can ignore competition within the 'general' market of the whole industry. If abnormally large profits are being earned in any branch of a competitive industry, the firms earning them will face keen competition not only from new firms entering the industry from outside, but also from firms in other, perhaps overcrowded, sections of the industry itself.

This keenness of competition is similar in intensity, though different in type, to that where products are identical. With competition between the many producers of a homogeneous product, there is merely *price competition*; the essence of the competitive struggle is to produce exactly the same product more economically, and therefore more cheaply, than other firms. With competition between firms which do *not* make identical goods, there are many other forms of competitive activity in which firms can indulge.

First, firms can alter the physical nature of their products—they can 'differentiate' them. If they think it worth while, producers may increase their profits by changing the constituents, the design or the wrapping of their products, rather than by changing prices. In such an industry, therefore, there will be frequent changes in the nature of their own product by 'innovating' firms which have discovered a variant on their existing design that has a greater appeal for consumers. Such alterations will soon induce changes in the products of 'run-of-the-mill' producers who hope to cash in on the 'innovator's' profits. Meanwhile, the innovator himself may have decided on a further change. It is by alterations of this kind that competition through product differentiation keeps all producers alert and efficient.

There may, however, be considerable differences between the products of the various broad sections of the whole industry, based perhaps on different methods of production. For example, the ladies' dressmaking trade has three broad sections. First, there are firms producing high-class garments. Second, there are firms producing standard machine-made dresses, but with an individual worker making the whole garment. Third, there are factories making mass-produced dresses, where the division of labour is considerable and each girl performs only one operation before passing on the garment to the next worker. The high-class trade will be carried out by small firms, with their own particular clientele. The elasticity of demand for the product will be rather low, the market small and prices high. In the 'machine-made' section, the firms where individual workers make the whole garment will not normally sell direct to the final customer, but will nevertheless have a relatively limited market and will charge relatively high prices. Finally, the mass-produced garments will come from the larger firms in the industry. These will have considerable markets (often through chain stores), a relatively high elasticity of demand for the product and low prices intended to capture a mass market.

In this type of situation, competition will be keener within the various sections of the industry than between them. Nevertheless, high profits in any one section of the trade will invite competition from firms in others. For example, the border-line between 'high-class' mass-produced dresses and 'low-class garments made by individual machinists is by no means clear-cut. Actual or potential competition from other sections of the trade will ensure that profits in any given section can never become abnormally large.

Finally, it must be noted that product differentiation does not depend only on differences in the physical constitution of products. It depends just as much on the type of service given by the seller. For example, in the retail trade a customer will patronise a particular shop because he has not to walk very far to reach it ; because he feels that the attention he receives is somehow superior ; or because the proprietor is a personal friend. Especially in the retail trade, such 'conditions surrounding the sale of the product' are very important. It makes no difference that the products sold by the various shops are all physically identical if, in the eyes of customers, some shops are more conveniently situated or more attractive than others. For it is what the consumer thinks that is the crucial factor. Thus, the only shop in a particular area will be able to charge high prices for a given product, since shoppers would have to spend money on bus fares to buy that product from rivals in neighbouring towns or villages ; an 'exclusive' shop will charge high prices for all goods, and so on.

Nevertheless, there will generally be keen competition within such a competitive industry. Shops in isolated areas will find that their 'local monopolies' are continually threatened by free delivery services offered by shops in near-by towns. Again, the 'high-class' grocer, if his ability to charge high prices enables him to make large profits, will meet competition, not only from new entrants to the grocery trade, but also from 'self service' grocers. And both of these, in turn, will meet competition from chain stores, whose main fields of interest may well be in fields other than the sale of foodstuffs. Product differentiation certainly does not mean that competition is not keen.

A second type of competition which does not arise when all products in the industry are identical is competition through advertising. It is true that this kind of competitive industry *as a whole* may try to increase sales by advertising its produce.

'There is *no* substitute for wool', we are told. But such an industry can find no place for advertising intended to sell the product of one firm at the expense of another. Since all products are identical, there is no point in trying to persuade consumers that one firm sells a better product than another. Where products are not all identical, this is the essential aim of advertising. The producer uses advertising as an important weapon in support of his attempts at product differentiation. The intention is not usually to expand the sales of the whole industry—only those of a particular firm. The name which the advertiser tries to impress on consumers is not the name of the industry's general product but the name of his own firm or of his firm's particular brand.

Such advertisement has two main objectives. First, by persuading consumers that the product of his firm has that 'extra something', each producer tries to convince consumers that rival products are only remote substitutes for his own. In other words, he tries to lower the elasticity of demand for his own product so that he may be able to raise its price and not suffer any serious decline in sales. The aim is to create an 'individual' market for his product. Second, he attempts to increase the size of that market. If successful, the producer will be able either to sell much more of his product at the existing price, or a little more at a much higher price. In either instance he will improve his own competitive position at the expense of his rivals.

Such *persuasive advertising*—advertising intended to persuade the consumer to buy one good rather than another—is an important feature of the modern economy. But, again, it does little or nothing to reduce the keenness of competition. A clientele built up through competitive advertising can be stolen by similar advertising on the part of other firms. So the competitive struggle is perpetual, each firm trying all the time to improve its own position at the expense of rivals, and no firm succeeding for very long.

Third, we must allow more explicitly for changes in the nature of productive processes. It is true that, with an identical product in a competitive industry, the development of new processes represents an important force leading to increased efficiency. With differentiated products, however, this essential fact of product differentiation means that slight changes in production methods often yield considerable profits; and producers will always be seeking to discover and benefit from such improvements.

Let us now consider how output and price are fixed in firms

producing under such conditions. The main difference from a situation where products are identical lies in the nature of sales conditions. Instead of selling an identical good whose price is given by 'the market', producers now have some control over their own price. The degree of such control will, of course, differ. Where competition is keen, and the demand for the firm's product very elastic, a small increase in the firm's price will mean the loss of much custom; where competition is slight and demand not highly elastic, it will not. What happens depends, then, on the elasticity of demand for the firm's product. This elasticity will be lower when it has few competitors and higher when there are many.

The producer must therefore think carefully before deciding where to fix his price and his output. If he raises his output, not only may his costs per unit of output rise; his receipts *per unit* will inevitably fall, even though *total* receipts will rise if demand is elastic. (We assume here, of course, that when the firm lowers its price, it does not simultaneously alter the demand conditions for its product by increasing its advertising expenditure.) Nevertheless, the producer will still fix his price so that the output which he can sell at that price allows him to make money. As a first approximation, we may again say that he will fix his price and output so that, having allowed for the fall in price and the change in cost which occurs when his output increases, the difference between his total receipts and his total costs is at a maximum—profits are maximised.

This is, however, only a first approximation to the truth. As with identical products, there are several reasons why firms do not always attempt to 'maximise' profits. There are again reasons depending on the psychology of individual business-men and boards of directors. There are the constraints imposed by the structure of contemporary society and by the nature of cost and demand conditions. Firms may also feel that it is desirable to keep prices more stable than would be possible if they were to seek perpetually to make the largest possible profits. For example, a producer of ladies' dresses will normally fix his prices 'for the season'. However, now that not all products are identical, firms can and do change the quality of their products during that season. If in the first few weeks it seems that a mistake in pricing has been made, it is always possible to change, say, the material used in a given dress without altering the price.

Nor should the willingness of firms in this type of industry to charge high prices be underestimated. We all know only too well the sharp increase in the price of flowers just before Mothering Sunday, Christmas and Easter. Also, the fact that a competitive industry contains many small firms means that they have not the capital required to finance the piling up of stocks which would occur if they maintained their own prices whilst other firms were cutting theirs. Again, in view of the competitive nature of the industry, order books cannot be allowed to lengthen too far. Rivals will always be ready to compete for custom—at a price. In times of general inflation firms may increase their orders in hand rather than their prices; when conditions are more normal, competition for orders will make it more profitable to raise prices.

A further obstacle to earning the absolute maximum of profit is more serious. We have so far spoken as though each firm makes only one product. In fact most firms make many. It is thus not a simple matter to decide how to distribute the firm's overheads between the various products. In principle the answer is simple; each product should bear that proportion of total overheads which enables the firm to maximise profits. If a given product has a relatively low elasticity of demand, a high price for it will leave the amount demanded little affected. It should therefore bear a relatively large proportion of the firm's overheads; its price should be high. Similarly, a product which is in keen competition with those of other firms will have a high elasticity of demand, and should have a relatively low price, each unit of output bearing a relatively small proportion of the overheads. In other words, the principle of pricing should be to 'charge what the traffic will bear'.

If all firms knew exactly what the elasticity of demand for each of their products was, they would no doubt normally obey this principle. Since they do not know, they often tend to fall back on a 'rule of thumb'. To the direct (variable) costs of each product, they will add a certain margin to cover overheads. They then add a further percentage margin to allow for profits and obtain the 'full cost' of the product. This 'rule of thumb' might seem to mean that firms rarely maximise profits. In practice, however, the size of the 'conventional' profit margin contained in 'full cost' will depend broadly on underlying economic conditions. Long experience gives business-men the 'feel' of the trade and enables them to know fairly accurately 'what the market will bear'. Bradford worsted manufacturers, for example, may not have ever heard of the concept of elasticity of demand, but this does not prevent them from making consistent attempts to earn maximum profits. Further, in such an industry, competition is so keen that the firm will have little scope for charging other than the profit-maximising price, subject, of course, to the institutional and psychological qualifications discussed above. Keen competition again means that the 'margins of tolerance' within which each firm is forced to work are very small.

The above discussion has been entirely in terms of how to fix price and output, but it applies equally to decisions about the scale of expenditure on advertising and about the kind of product to make. Producers will attempt to make those particular products which will yield maximum profits. Similarly, with advertising, it will pay to go on increasing expenditure up to the point where the extra profits brought in by additional advertising no longer exceed the costs of such advertising. If this policy is followed, profits will be at a maximum.

Let us now study the effects of changes in economic conditions in a competitive industry where products are not all identical. We consider, first, the effect of an increased demand for the industry's product, and second, the impact of the introduction of new products and processes.

Where the demand for the product of a competitive industry producing differentiated products increases permanently and considerably, the result will be much the same as where products are identical. In the short period prices will rise. The prices of different firms' goods may, however, rise in different degrees. If the increased demand is mainly for goods consumed by the 'upper classes' of society, prices at the upper end of the scale will rise most. If it is working-class demand that has risen, the prices of cheaper goods will be most affected. In any event, all firms will increase output beyond the normal capacity level and both costs and prices will rise. The result will be that profits are abnormally high. If profits are relatively higher in some sections of the industry than in others, firms will tend to move from the less to the more profitable sections. But, in the long run, the main competition may come from outside the existing industry.

Entirely new firms will be set up; firms in other closely related industries will transfer their activities into the industry in question. This will lead, in the long period, to a new position where profits are again 'normal', the industry is larger, and, since there are more firms, a greater number of 'differentiated' products is being produced. In this final situation, as in the initial position, some firms will be losing money, some will be earning large profits, and some will just be covering their costs. The general level of profits will, however, be that which one would normally expect in such an industry, as will the rates of entry and exit of firms.

Finally, we consider what will happen when a completely new product is introduced into a competitive industry, for example, the impact of a new man-made fibre on a traditional textile industry. Let us assume that before this introduction takes place, the textile industry is in a situation where there is only a 'normal' rate of change in products and in processes. When the new material, say nylon, appears, a number of developments in final products will become possible, and consequent changes in processes will be needed.

Firms will have to discover how to spin the new fibre on existing cotton, woollen or worsted machinery. They will have to overcome problems of knitting and weaving it, for example, how to eliminate static electricity. They will also have to discover economical and attractive methods of dyeing and finishing. Those firms which are able most quickly to discover how best to use the properties of the new fibre in final products, and how to process it most readily, will reap considerable short-term profits before other firms learn such secrets for themselves. There will be a spate of new products and processes, as firms attempt to reap the profits which await successful 'innovators'.

Nor will these developments be the prerogative of the larger and better-known firms in the industry. The more spectacular 'technical' developments may come from the bigger firms. But in solving the more ordinary problems, all firms, big and small, will make their own contribution. Even firms from outside the industry may be concerned. For example, chemical firms may interest themselves in the problems of dyeing nylon.

For a time, therefore, there will be abnormally high profits in the sections of the textile industry using the new fibre. In the long run, however, these abnormal profits will be competed away by the inflow of new firms, new products and new processes; a situation will be reached where the rate at which new products are introduced returns to 'normal', and this will persist until some fresh technical development begins the whole process of innovation afresh.

This chapter has dealt with competition of two kinds: first, where many firms produce a homogeneous product; second, where they produce differentiated products. We may note, in conclusion, that economists refer to the first type of competition as 'pure' or 'perfect'. The second they call 'monopolistic competition'. For whilst each firm has a 'monopoly' of its own product, all products compete in the industry's 'general' market.

CHAPTER IV

MONOPOLY

WE have already made the distinction between competition, where many firms produce goods that are close substitutes for each other, and monopoly, where such substitutes are few and remote. This distinction corresponds to that made in ordinary parlance; but it is not quite adequate here. We shall find it worth while distinguishing monopoly in the strict sense, where there is *only a single monopolist* producing any given product, from situations where there is more than one producer of the good in question, but still only a small number. This latter situation, where a few firms each sell a considerable proportion of the output of a product, is known to economists as 'oligopoly'. Just as an oligarchy means a small group of men ruling a country, so an oligopoly comprises a small number of firms all producing the same, or very similar, products. In everyday speech one normally includes both 'true' monopoly and oligopoly under the word monopoly; we shall here distinguish them carefully. For the problems and policies of producers will be very different in the two situations.

We first consider monopoly. A monopolist is the sole producer of a given product, so that we need consider only the individual firm. In a real sense the firm and the industry are one. For example, the firm T. M. M. Ltd. are the makers of some 90 per cent of the cotton and worsted spinning machinery produced in Britain. For all practical purposes, T. M. M. *is* the British cotton- and worsted-spinning machinery industry.

The predominant feature which distinguishes monopoly from competition is that the kinds of constraint which the individual producer faces by virtue of the keen rivalry in a competitive industry disappear. There is little need for a monopolist to pursue either maximum efficiency or maximum profits merely because he fears that otherwise his rivals will drive him out of business. He has no close rivals. His room for manœuvre, whilst not unlimited, is far greater than under competition. It

follows that the policy of a monopolist is simultaneously less cir-
cumscribed and less predictable than that of a competitive firm.

The way in which the individual firm fixes its price and
output will be the same, in principle, whether there is competition or monopoly. The business-man will still fix his output
and his profit margin so as to maximise profit, subject to the
qualifications outlined in Chapter II; but the size of that profit
margin will tend to differ considerably. Economists are agreed
that, in general, the profits earned by a monopolist will be quite
large. Certainly the ordinary citizen automatically connects
monopoly with high profits. The absence of competition is considered to be an open invitation both to high prices and profits.
It is also probable that the output of a monopolist will be smaller
than one might expect in a competitive industry. As we have
seen, the demand for his product tends to be inelastic. An
increase in sales may well reduce total receipts and yet is certain
to increase total costs. It will therefore pay any monopolist, if
he is producing at a level of output where demand is inelastic,
to restrict output until demand becomes so elastic that any
further rise in price would lower receipts more than it reduced
costs.

The essential difference between competition and monopoly
is that new factors become important in determining prices and
output. In politically advanced countries the fear of nationalisation, government control, or the artificial stimulation of competition directed against him, may influence a monopolist's price
policy. Public opinion may be able to bring about the introduction of controls over a firm which it regards as having abused
its monopoly power by earning large profits. Nor, of course, is
it a solution to allow economic and technical inefficiency to eat
up potential profits, thereby avoiding public censure and control.
Inefficiency, resulting from lack of competition, is another fault
commonly imputed to the monopolist and is often considered as
a good reason for nationalisation or for the deliberate creation of
competition.

It should perhaps be made clear that to mention the monopolist's fear of antagonising public opinion does not imply that
the term monopoly applies only to large, well-known firms. It
is true that such firms alone are likely to be seriously considered
as candidates for nationalisation or government-created competition. However, even the less spectacular monopolist will not
wish to arouse public resentment. For example, consider the

D

caterer who supplies refreshments to a cricket-match crowd on a hot day. It would be hard to find any alternative source of refreshment without leaving the cricket ground—which would mean paying again to return. If, as is likely on a hot day, the demand for cooling drinks is highly inelastic, 'monopoly profits' could be earned by charging high prices. Even so, the caterer has to be careful of pressing his advantage too far. Quite apart from the purely economic fact that if prices are raised very far even the thirst-parched cricket enthusiasts will go without a drink —the demand for drinks will become *elastic*—the caterer is unlikely to run the risk of antagonising his customers by charging what are regarded as 'excessive' prices. However trivial his monopoly may be, no monopolist dare maximise his profits at the cost of public ill-will in a world where monopoly and exploitation of the consumer are frequently regarded as synonymous.

A further possibility is that the monopolist may fail to maximise his profits because he feels that high prices are in some moral sense 'unfair'. It is, of course, extremely hard to distinguish between pure kind-heartedness or moral scruples and the fear of arousing public anger of the kind just considered. One suspects that monopolists are more often benevolent through compulsion (real or imagined) than through free choice. Nevertheless, pure kind-heartedness, though undoubtedly rare, cannot be completely ruled out. In a competitive industry, any predilection to benevolence is overshadowed by the overriding need to keep abreast of one's competitors. In monopoly the producer's foibles can be indulged. The very absence of competition which gives the monopolist the chance to exploit his customers also allows him to pamper them.

Finally, an important factor influencing the monopolist's price-output policy is his fear of potential competition. A highly profitable monopoly, by making other business-men's mouths water, represents a strong force attracting new firms to enter the field. No monopolist will dare to ignore this possibility that excessive greed on his part will merely make it more certain than ever that he will attract the competition of rivals.

The extent of this danger of attracting competition will depend on the source of the monopolist's power. In some cases technical factors will be the foundation of monopoly, in the sense that the smallest possible production unit can easily supply the whole market. Such a 'natural' monopoly will not be easy to break. But the most widespread basis of monopoly to-day undoubtedly lies in institutional factors like patents and trade-marks. In such circumstances, it is never possible to be certain how safe one's monopoly is. Patents, for example, do not last for ever, and may not represent a complete protection even whilst they do last. Certainly, for a monopolist to rely on institu-tional supports to earn large profits is to invite competitors to find loopholes in his legal protection, or to find ways of producing close substitutes for his product without even apparently breaking the law. The best and most profitable course may therefore be to preserve the monopoly by being content with reasonable prices and a moderate return over a period of years. A policy of trying to earn as much as possible for a short period of time may lead to a price war brought about because these high returns attract new entrants into the monopolist's market.

The safest conclusion about monopoly is that there is no simple explanation of monopoly policy. No satisfactory solution can be precise and clear-cut in a situation where the individual producer, by the lack of competition, has so much freedom of action and so many possible policies. However, the various policies outlined above seem to cover all the most likely circum-stances.

Finally, it is worth stressing again the fact that, in the eco-nomic sense, a monopolist need not be in control of a nation-wide or a world-wide market. Such monopolies do exist ; but there are also many smaller 'monopolies' where a single firm has control over a local market. Though unimportant from a national point of view, such a monopoly may be extremely important to its own customers. Monopolistic exploitation can be as important to a village in its dealings with the local cobbler or grocer as in the world market for precious stones or rare and essential minerals. For, after allowing for the restraints which any monopolist suffers from, he may still be able to earn considerable profits ; and this may well cause much alarm and heart-searching in the short run. In the long run, however, even if there is no political control over such a monopolist, his monopoly position is likely to be weakened by the entry of new firms and by the introduction of the new products and processes of production which between them comprise Professor Schumpeter's 'gale of creative de-struction'. Old products and processes are destroyed and replaced by new ones.

If one turns from monopoly to oligopoly, the problems become more rather than less difficult. The monopolist can at least plan his activities secure in the knowledge that, whilst in the long run it may attract new firms to his field, nothing he does in the short run will provoke serious reactions from his competitors— for he has none. The oligopolist has. What is more, any change in the price charged by one oligopolist will almost automatically cause changes in the prices charged by the others; these latter changes in turn will react back on the original price-cutter; and the price-cutter's next move may start a serious 'price war'. For, since each firm produces a large proportion of the output of the whole industry, one cannot assume, as in competition, that a change in the price and output of the individual firm has negligible effects on the price and output of the industry as a whole. This is, indeed, the basic feature of oligopoly. No firm dare make any move without first considering all its likely results. More- over, the smallness of the number of firms in any 'oligopolistic' industry means that both the originators and the effects of any competitive price changes are all too obvious. Competition in oligopoly is often more acrimonious and aggressive than in a competitive market, where the considerable number of firms makes competition largely an impersonal phenomenon.

A typical instance of aggressive competition in oligopoly is the 'war' between the producers of household detergents in post-war Britain. The essentials of the struggle have been as follows. First, the key feature has been a nation-wide advertising campaign of an aggressive nature. The aim has been to 'differ- entiate' the various products sufficiently to convince consumers that the one in question performs the same service as the others —but much more efficiently.

Second, the 'list prices' of packets of the various detergents have remained both constant and identical for long periods. There has been no 'price war' in the sense of competitive cutting of list prices. But so many reduced price vouchers and free samples have been handed out that only a very small proportion of sales can have taken place at the officially advertised prices. The advantage of such a policy is that not only can a direct 'price war', with all its dangers and administrative inconvenience, be avoided; at the same time rival firms will find it impossible to calculate what the prices *actually* charged by their rivals to consumers have been.

Aggressive advertising; product differentiation; 'under-the- counter' price cutting, often combined with constant, even identical, list prices—these are the characteristics of the keen battles that typify oligopoly. But no war, commercial or military, lasts for ever. All oligopolistic struggles end sooner or later, usually in an actual or tacit agreement between the 'belligerents'. It is possible, of course, that one firm may be so obviously set for victory that it is able to take over the other firms and turn oligopoly into monopoly. However, an agreement which regulates the future relations between the oligopolists whilst preserving their independence is more likely. In some cases, an actual written agreement may be entered into; but there is the danger that such an agreement may be considered illegal—especially in countries with strong anti-monopoly legislation. As a result, many oligopoly agreements are unwritten; they may be based on verbal 'gentlemen's agreements', or merely on a tacit understanding, where firms voluntarily avoid taking any action which would be likely to begin a 'war' between them.

Where the number of firms in the industry is very small, less than, say, six or seven, an actual agreement, written or unwritten, is likely to be reached, though such periods of agreement and truce will often be interrupted by a short-lived war which will end either in a further agreement or in outright control over the industry by one firm.

If there is a fair number of firms—say twenty or thirty—any concrete agreement will be difficult to achieve and, of course, ultimately oligopoly will shade imperceptibly into competition as the number of firms in the industry becomes larger.

Where no actual agreement is possible because there are too many firms, or where any agreement is illegal, one will find a type of policy noted by many economists who have carried out actual case studies. This is the policy of having 'a quiet life'. The prices charged by all the firms in an oligopolistic group will remain constant unless there are substantial changes in the underlying economic conditions. Thus a given level of prices may be maintained for months, even years, because no firm feels that it dare make the first move towards a change. For an oligopolist will often feel that if he raises his price his competitors will be unlikely to alter theirs, so that he will lose much custom. Again, if he lowers his price, he will fear that his rivals will lower their prices so that he will not expand his sales significantly. This fear, that any change will be for the worse, may well explain why, in oligopoly, prices often remain unaltered for long periods.

A price rise will occur only if there is, say, a substantial increase in costs. Then all firms in the industry will be prepared either to raise prices by mutual consent or else to follow the action of a 'price leader' and raise their prices similarly. Again, a price reduction may take place if, for example, there is a substantial fall in raw material prices. All the firms may feel that there is room for making price reductions without running a serious risk of starting a 'cut-throat' price war.

If this idea that oligopolists often wish to live, and indeed succeed in living, a 'quiet life' is reasonable, it means that profits may not be maximised. If there is an actual agreement between oligopolists, the most sensible policy may be for them to act like a single monopolist, to 'maximise industry profits' and then share out the spoils between themselves. If such an agreement does not exist, the resulting policy of 'playing safe' and enjoying a peaceful life may well fail to result in maximum profits, either for the individual firm or for the whole industry. Nevertheless, it is an attractive idea, reinforced by a study of actual oligopolistic industries, that so long as profits in an industry continue to be 'reasonable' or 'fair', there will be no desire on the part of any oligopolist to change prices. No one will wish to court the disaster of a price war merely in an attempt to make the, perhaps relatively small, changes needed to maximise his profits. Above all, in this situation, there is the great difficulty that no firm can know what the demand conditions for his own product are unless he makes assumptions about his rivals' price policy. And the uncertainties about the rivals' response to any price cut, and about its exact results on the demand for one's own product, are so great that inactivity is often a desirable state whenever profits are reasonably good. Price alterations are therefore unlikely except in times of considerable change in the underlying situation. In any case, the oligopolist can always rely on advertising and product differentiation, provided this is not of a too acrimonious nature, to achieve relatively small improvements in his profits without any danger of a real 'battle'.

It follows from this discussion that both monopoly and oligopoly are prone to mean high prices and profits, since keen competition, of the kind where there are many small firms in an industry, is absent. It has also often been held that monopoly is likely to mean productive inefficiency, since there is no competitive spur to technical progress. No generalisation is possible, however. It is certain that there will be no automatic competitive stimulus to technical efficiency, but the monopolist may be impelled to efficiency either by his desire to show potential competitors that they will not find his firm an easy prey, or by the fear that, if the inefficiency of his firm becomes too obvious, public opinion will lead to some kind of public supervision or control. He may even *enjoy* being progressive.

In oligopoly there is much less danger of technical backwardness. The very fierceness of competition during periods of 'war' means that firms will regard technical efficiency as one of the few safe insurances against disaster if the competitive struggle is renewed. Moreover, the fact that in periods of 'peace' oligopoly profits will be comfortably large (partly because the firms themselves are large) means that they have adequate resources to finance the expensive research and development schemes that are so typical of modern industry. Indeed, it may even be that oligopoly is the most progressive form of industrial organisation today. Since 'price competition' is often ruled out, 'technological competition' may occur instead. Firms will attempt to improve their productive techniques more rapidly than their rivals. In the short run this will enable them to make larger profits and yet not lower prices. In the long run it may so improve their competitive efficiency as to make them ready, and indeed willing, to lower prices, even if this results in a 'price war'. On the other hand, it will also make them stronger to fight a 'war' begun by someone else. Such 'technological competition' may therefore represent a real spur to technical efficiency in oligopoly; at the same time the firms are likely to be large and prosperous enough to be able to spend considerable sums of money on plant, equipment and research. On the other hand, a competitive industry with many small firms might lack the resources to carry out research and development—except through a research centre financed by the whole industry.

One type of monopolistic organisation not so far mentioned is the 'cartel'. Here, a number of firms, perhaps many quite small firms, join together in a purely *selling* monopoly organisation. Each firm has complete control over its own production processes; but the selling prices, and sometimes the actual amount of goods which each firm is allowed to sell, are centrally controlled by the cartel. Economists are in general agreement that a cartel will be less efficient, and will charge higher prices, than a single monopolist. Since the cartel's production is not organised centrally but left to each individual firm, there is no likelihood that the advantages of large-scale production, which a 'real' monopolist can possess, will be found in a cartel.

The only circumstances in which a cartel is likely to represent a desirable form of organisation is where there is a severe slump in an industry with keen competition and much capital equipment. Total unit costs will then greatly exceed *direct* costs per unit of output, and firms may find it profitable to go on selling below full unit costs, provided only that their *direct* cost per unit of output is covered. There may therefore be ruinous 'weak selling' in the industry. Yet there may also be too many firms for them to agree tacitly (as can happen in oligopoly) to close down altogether once prices are not sufficient to cover full unit costs, in order to avoid 'spoiling the market'.

In these conditions, which existed in some sections of the Lancashire cotton industry during the 1930's, a cartel may be positively desirable. It can keep up prices and give some degree of stability and prosperity to the industry, thereby allowing the capital equipment which is in excess of the community's long-term requirements to leave the industry in an 'orderly' way. The inevitable snag, of course, is that the rate at which members of the cartel are prepared for such 'orderly elimination of capacity' to take place is usually much slower than that which an impartial observer would think fit. There is hence a danger that the cartel may charge high prices to bolster up a declining industry.

CHAPTER V

WAGES

HAVING seen how the prices of the products sold in the modern community are fixed, we must now discover how the rewards of the various factors of production are determined. We begin with what for many of us is the most important reward—the wage, or salary, of labour. Later, we must consider the returns to the non-human factors of production, like land, machinery and money.

In the present chapter, we shall consider in particular the earnings of manual workers engaged in industry. The argument can fairly easily be applied also to non-manual workers and to those engaged in farming and commerce. We shall concentrate our attention here on the way in which wages in individual industries are determined. We shall show the main characteristics of the demand and supply of labour in individual industries and thus explain how differences in wages between different industries, occupations and areas arise. The way in which the *general level* of money wages is determined will be considered later, in Chapter IX.

As always, our problem resolves itself into a question of demand and supply. If the general level of money wages is taken for the moment as given, differences in wages between occupations and industries must depend on the particular characteristics of demand and supply in those given fields.

An individual industry will demand labour for the fundamental reason that labour is *productive*. Each individual employer in the trade will hire labour only because he knows that such labour can be set to work, using the firm's capital equipment, to produce goods for sale to consumers or to other entrepreneurs. The demand for labour is thus 'derived' from the ultimate demand for consumption or capital goods. On the assumption that business-men aim at maximum profits, it follows that the number of men employed by any individual firm will be such that the firm's profits are at a maximum. This is merely another way of saying that a firm will normally fix its *output* so as to maximise its profits. For, given the short-run size and nature of its buildings and machinery, a firm can only change its output by altering the size or the composition of its labour force.

On the basis of such an assumption about the behaviour of individual firms, it is possible to make reasonable generalisations about the nature of the demand for labour in any individual industry. In the short run, the matter is simple. The size of each individual firm will be fixed and the number of firms in the industry will not be able to vary greatly. As a result, the number of workers employed by any industry will be smaller the higher the wage that has to be paid to them, and vice versa. For, with its given capital equipment, a firm will be able to expand its output beyond the normal capacity level only if it is prepared to suffer a falling-off in the average productivity of its workers. Even if there is no change in the innate ability of workers, the fact that more of them are employed will mean an over-intensive use of its capital equipment. Workers will, for instance, have too little 'elbow-room', output per man will fall off and the wage which the firm can afford to pay will decline too. Thus, both in the individual firm and in the industry as a whole, with given demand conditions for the industry's product, more workers will be employed in the short period if wages are low, and fewer workers if wages are high.

In the long run, there is less certainty about the nature of the industry's demand for labour. It is no longer obvious that productivity per worker must decline as the size of the industry's labour force increases. In the individual firm, it may be possible (though this is perhaps rare) to increase the size of the plant and the amount of machinery, and thus to allow an enlarged labour force to attain the same level of productivity per worker as with a smaller labour force. Again, even if it is impossible for individual firms to expand in size without suffering a decline in labour productivity, the labour force of the industry may be able to expand indefinitely at the same level of productivity, because new firms come into the industry and operate at a level of efficiency equal to that already attained by the existing firms.

If either of the above conditions were fulfilled, firms would be able to take on more workers without any decline in productivity. Wages would consequently be able to remain constant as employment expanded. In practice, however, there will be

other factors which will ensure that more workers can be employed by an industry, even in the long run, only if wages fall;
for in practice an increase in employment in an industry is
normally associated with a fall in the average productivity of
labour. In the first place, as the industry expands it is likely
that both the workers and the employers who now enter it will
be less efficient than those already there. The general level of
labour productivity in the industry will decline, partly because
incoming workers are less able than those already in the industry,
and partly because the incoming business-men are themselves
less capable of using the labour they employ to the best advantage.
This, of course, emphasises the important point that the productivity of labour depends to some extent on the efficiency with
which individual managements direct it, and on the efficiency of
the machinery which it uses.

Yet perhaps the most important reason why an increase in
the number of workers employed in a given industry will, even
in the long run, be possible only if wages fall is that the individual
industry will be able to sell more of its product if, but only if,
the price of its product falls relatively to the prices of other
products. Only if the price of the good produced by the industry
falls can income and substitution effects lead consumers to buy
more of the good in question—and perhaps less of others. So,
even if output per man remains constant, in terms of actual
physical output produced, the price of the industry's product
will fall. This will inevitably mean that manufacturers cannot
afford to expand their labour forces unless wages fall too.

Our fundamental and common-sense proposition is therefore
unassailable. An individual industry will employ more workers
if, but only if, wages fall. Similarly, an increase in the wages
received by an industry's workers will lower the level of employment in that industry.

All that has been said here, of course, applies only to a situation where the demand conditions for the individual industry's
product remain constant. What will be the effect on wages if
demand conditions alter is a question which must be considered
later. For the moment let us use the information we have
obtained to explain differences in wages between industries and
occupations.

We have seen that the usefulness of labour to employers
depends partly on its physical productivity—on the amount of
actual physical output it produces—and partly on the price at

which that physical output can be sold. The first of these factors is probably more important in explaining differences in wages between occupations, and the second in explaining differences between industries. In both cases, however, the nature of the supply conditions for labour will represent an additional and important factor.

Let us first consider differences in the wages paid in different occupations. To take the most general case; why are the wages of skilled workers higher than those of ordinary labourers? Much of the explanation lies, as we have seen, in differences in productivity. The skilled worker is more 'productive'. This does not mean that he will necessarily produce more physical units of output. In a world where the division of labour is an essential feature of industrial activity, it is, in any case, rare for a worker to produce the whole of any product himself. But skilled workers will usually be more 'productive' in the sense that they make a more vital contribution to industrial activity than do ordinary unskilled labourers.

It is hard, however, to separate this superior productivity on the part of skilled workers from the conditions of their supply. Except perhaps in times of slump, skilled labour tends to be scarcer (and therefore automatically more expensive) than ordinary unskilled labour. Not every one is fitted, willing or able to spend the time and money needed to acquire industrial skills; but anyone can take an unskilled job. To some extent, then, the greater productivity of the skilled worker is a direct result of his 'scarcity'. If there were larger numbers of skilled men and women, their individual contributions to industry would seem less vital. Nevertheless, the fact that the productivity of skilled workers is higher cannot be denied—and it is this difference in productivity which explains why their wages are higher than those of unskilled workers.

Having explained why *in general* skilled workers will earn more than unskilled ones, we may note an important reason why particular types of skilled worker will earn unusually high wages. This may, of course, be a result of unusually high productivity; in practice, however, the most obvious instances of very high wages are those where there is a deliberate restriction in the supply of labour—which automatically raises its price. Especially where there is a strong trade union, workers in a particular trade may restrict the number of entrants into that trade—as may have happened, for example, in the British printing trade. The result is obvious. Given an individual industry's demand for labour of a particular kind, the smaller the number of men of that type who are 'supplied', the higher will be the wage which their employers are prepared to offer them.

Differences in wages between *industries* may also be a result of differences in productivity and skill. In the medical profession, where skill is great and expensive to acquire, salaries will be higher than in, say, refuse collection, where no special skill is needed. However, the most interesting examples of differences in wages between industries occur where differences in wages are the result of differences in the prosperity—and hence the price level —in the particular industries. For example, in Britain in the second half of the nineteenth century, agriculture was declining, whilst manufacturing industry was growing. Consequently, abstracting entirely from any differences in the physical productivity of labour, wages were low in agriculture where prices were low, and higher in manufacturing where prices were higher. Similarly, between 1920 and 1939, wages in the British coal and cotton industries were kept down by depressed trade; in the expanding light-engineering industries wages were relatively high.

Once again, the problem of supply enters the situation. Even where there is little difference between the skills required in the declining and the expanding industries, workers will not readily change their jobs—which often means changing their home towns. The supply of labour in the 'declining areas' remains high, despite low wages. Where the declining industry is one which requires particular skills, the problem is even more acute. The labour in, say, the cotton industry, is highly trained in a particular specialist task—it is 'specific' to that industry. It is therefore hard to induce workers to leave the cotton industry and find jobs, say, in engineering factories, even in the same town. Low wages in cotton will fail to reduce the supply of the 'specific' labour very substantially, and wages are therefore likely to fall to extremely low levels. Similarly, a scarcity of 'specific' labour in an expanding industry, for example in post-war British radio manufacture, will mean that wages are even higher than the mere fact of the prosperity of the industry would have meant in itself.

Similar factors will explain differences in wages between different areas. A town composed mainly of professional men will have a higher wage level than one of agricultural labourers. An area containing only declining industries will have lower wages than one which is prosperous and expanding. Above all, one must remember that even today, with nation-wide markets for consumer goods and nation-wide trade unions, there is no such thing as a nation-wide labour market. Quite apart from the fact that workers are usually not particularly well-informed about wages and working conditions outside their own particular district, it is often both expensive and unpleasant to leave one's own trade and one's home town to seek a better wage elsewhere. Thus, even in a country like modern Britain, there can be considerable differences in wages from area to area, the exact size of the differences depending on existing conditions of demand and supply in the various local markets.

We have mentioned the supply of labour frequently in the above analysis of wage differentials, and it will pay us to consider it in more detail. During the eighteenth and nineteenth centuries it was often held that the supply conditions of labour were such, both in individual industries and in the whole economy, that wages could never rise above the level required for a bare minimum of subsistence. The 'Iron Law of Wages' was held to mean that if wages were to rise above this minimum level there would soon be so great an increase in the size of the population that wages would be driven down, once again, to the minimum necessary for a bare existence. In other words, it was felt that workers would take advantage of any rise in wages, however small, to increase the size of their families and not to raise the standard of life of the existing members of these families.

So whilst wages might rise above the subsistence level where the special skills needed in a trade or restrictions on entry into that trade made it possible, the *general* level of wages would remain always very close to the minimum of subsistence. In such a world, any attempts of trade unions and philanthropists to raise wages could be relied upon to founder because of rising birth rates and falling death rates. There are indications that a situation of this kind still prevails in countries like India and China; in Western Europe, however, its days are over. Workers will not automatically take advantage of a rise in wages to increase the size of their families. General wage rates *can* rise above the 'bare subsistence minimum'.

From the point of view of the individual industry, the main factor determining the minimum wage that it must pay today to attract any workers at all will not be the 'subsistence minimum'. The industry will need to pay an amount of money just sufficient to prevent workers from taking jobs in other industries. This, of course, merely begs the question. For what determines the minimum wage that the other industries must pay ? There is no clear-cut answer to this. There will be a *highly conventional* subsistence minimum wage—perhaps related to the rate of unemployment pay—below which trade-union agitation, strikes and labour unrest will cause the labour supply to dry up. Fortunately the question is largely academic ; wages are rarely pushed down to such abysmal levels in Western Europe.

Where wages in the individual industry have risen above this minimum level, the behaviour of the supply of labour is less easy to predict. If wages rise, the number of hours of work done will increase in some cases but diminish in others. With goods, of course, the supply will practically always increase if the price of the good rises ; it will hardly ever diminish. This generalisation has led to a so-called 'law of supply and demand'. But the 'law' does not seem to apply to labour. If wages go up, the supply of labour sometimes rises and sometimes falls. For instance, many economists and others claim that a rise in the wages of, say, coal-miners is likely to reduce the supply of labour to the coal industry, because of an increase in 'voluntary absenteeism'.

Such behaviour may seem a little paradoxical, but it can be analysed, more rigorously and accurately than unaided common sense would allow if we use the kind of analysis worked out by economists for studying the reactions of consumers to changes in the prices of ordinary consumer goods. We can analyse a change in the worker's 'demand' for leisure, as an example of a 'price effect'. For the results of an increased wage rate depend on an 'income effect' on the one hand, and on a 'substitution effect' on the other. A rise in the wage rate represents a price effect, because income has become 'cheaper', whilst total time at the worker's disposal remains unaltered, so that his 'real income' rises. This is exactly analogous to the price effect studied in Chapter I (page 1) where the price of a single consumption good fell, whilst the consumer's money income remained constant.

The 'price effect' of a rise in wage rates will first include an income effect. The rise in wages per hour *must* make the worker better off, regardless of whether he works longer or shorter hours than before. For if he works exactly the same number of hours, he will have the same amount of leisure ; and yet his money income will have gone up, because the wage per hour has risen. The worker can therefore decide whether to take out the increased *real* income in the shape of an increased *money* income, an increased amount of leisure—or both. In practice, a worker will always increase the amount of his *money* income, and probably the amount of his leisure also, as a result of the income effect. This assumes, of course, that he is free to vary the amount of work he does. On the other hand, the price effect will also contain a substitution effect. The rise in wages will make leisure 'dearer' in terms of wages. Instead of sacrificing only, say, four shillings by taking an extra hour's leisure, the worker will now have to give up, say, five shillings.

Let us begin by looking at the substitution effect. As with any ordinary consumer good, the 'pure' substitution effect always works in only one direction : it induces the worker to 'buy' more of the good which has become relatively cheaper. In other words, so far as the substitution effect alone is concerned, the coal-miner will want to earn more wages each week by taking less leisure. We can isolate the 'pure' substitution effect if we suppose that, his hourly wage having been raised, the miner has a lump-sum, 'poll' tax imposed on him, of an amount just sufficient to prevent the rise in wage rates from making him, on balance, any better off than before. In this situation, the worker's *real* income will be no higher than previously ; but leisure is now 'dearer'. This means that the 'price' of an hour's leisure is now higher compared with other consumer goods, and the worker will consequently decide to cut down the amount of leisure he takes. He will 'substitute' other goods for leisure, now that the latter is relatively 'dearer'.

If a rise in wage rates induces a worker to take *more* leisure, this cannot be because of the substitution effect. It must be due to the income effect. We can isolate the 'pure' income effect by supposing that instead of his wage per hour being raised, a miner's elderly aunt has bequeathed to him a post-office savings-bank account. This pays him interest at regular intervals which he spends on consumption goods. Previously the miner's only source of money income had been work. He is now made 'better off' by the bequest, without the 'price' of leisure being changed at all. This is the 'pure' income effect. Now that he is more affluent, the miner may well, as common sense would suggest, decide to work less hard and to take more leisure. He may, for example, spend more time sitting in the sunshine.

We can now return to the price effect. The miner's aunt has

not left him a bequest; his hourly wages have risen. The substitution effect of this will certainly make the worker want to
work longer hours; the income effect will most probably make
him want to work shorter hours. For his *real* income has risen,
and this is almost certain to make him want more leisure as well
as a bigger *money* income to spend on ordinary consumer goods.

When we analysed the consumer's response to a fall in the
price of a single good in Chapter I, it was reasonable to assume
that the substitution effect was stronger than the income effect.
With a rise in hourly wages the situation is different. A miner's
money income is normally derived solely from his earnings as a
hewer of coal. A change in his rate of wages is therefore bound
to have a much larger effect on his real income than would the
same proportionate change in the price of any single consumer
good which he buys. The income effect will therefore probably
be very strong; and it may well predominate over the substitution effect. And, whilst the substitution effect will always represent an inducement for a worker to work *more* hours, the income
effect will tend to induce him to work fewer hours. Consequently
the *net* result of a rise in wage rates can easily be that the worker
works fewer hours and enjoys more leisure than when his wage
per hour was lower.

The true picture is a little complicated by the fact that leisure
is not always spent idly sitting in the sun. It is sometimes spent
in expensive visits to football matches or cinemas. Again, workers
may buy television sets which can be enjoyed only during leisure
hours at home, and not during working hours. A rise in wage
rates will therefore mean increased purchases of some goods
which are purchased with money in the ordinary way. To this
extent, the worker will not 'buy' more leisure at the expense of
reducing his weekly earnings. If he wants to spend his leisure
enjoying expensive consumer goods, he must first earn enough
money to buy them. On the other hand, it is certainly no use
working hard to buy 'luxuries' if one then has no leisure in which
to enjoy them. This is an acute dilemma which confronts many
business and professional men in the 'higher income groups'.
There is also the added complication that wives and families
sometimes have strong views both about what the family ought
to buy and also about the leisure hours which the 'bread winner'
should take. The family may indeed be able to influence his
behaviour. When decisions are made 'collectively' in this way,
no universally valid generalisation seems possible.

E

It should, however, be pointed out that this analysis of the probable effects of rising earnings on hours of work is not a mere intellectual toy, invented by economic theorists for their own amusement. It is a matter of great practical importance. Wage rates have risen markedly during the first half of the twentieth century; hours of work have fallen no less markedly. This implies that workers in the Western world now prefer to take advantage of a rise in real income caused by higher wage rates to reduce their hours of work and not only to raise their money incomes. Both these changes have transformed the living standards of millions of people, and it seems likely that the reduction in hours of work is a result of the rise in wage rates. Certainly, trade unions in Western Europe and America seem to have welcomed the opportunity, during the last fifty years, to press strongly for a progressively shorter working week. This willingness of trade unions to press for shorter hours has depended in turn on the willingness of the individual members of trade unions to reduce hours of work rather than to earn more money.

This leads us back to the rôle of trade unions and to their influence on the level of wages. The main objective of trade unions, of course, is to negotiate with employers for higher wages, and often for better working conditions. The extent to which, if we concentrate our attention on wages, unions are able to raise wages in any industry will depend largely on the nature of competition in that industry. If an industry is highly competitive, the initial result of the formation of a trade union may well be to increase the general level of wages. Provided that the agreement covers the whole of the industry, hard-hearted employers, who previously paid wages below the general level to their 'sweated' labour, may now find themselves forced to raise their wage payments to the general level. The formation of an apparently monopolistic organisation like a trade union may thus reduce the extent of discrimination in the labour market, and ensure that all workers of the same type receive the same wage. Thus far, the result of the action of the trade union would be unequivocally beneficial. But if an attempt were now made to raise wages further, it is likely that the number of workers employed would decline. Since the industry is highly competitive, profits will be small; the least efficient workers cannot be kept after wages have risen; and employment will fall. It is perfectly true that, if the demand for the industry's product is highly inelastic, it will be possible to increase prices without much difficulty and thereby keep the reduction in employment to a minimum. But employment is bound to fall, however slightly.

This raises a serious issue for the trade union in a competitive industry, for it has to choose between higher wage rates and a higher level of employment. Is it preferable to increase the wages of those workers who remain employed at the expense of sending other men out of work? This difficult choice is always present for the trade union in a competitive industry. Unions have to operate within fairly narrow limits in a highly competitive industry.

Even so, the actual level of wages will not be easy to predict in advance. It cannot fall below the subsistence minimum; nor can it rise above the level that labour productivity in the industry warrants, without reducing profits below the level needed to maintain a 'normal' rate of entry of new firms into the industry. It seems likely that wages will be nearer the lower limit in time of depression and nearer the upper limit in times of boom, for the simple reason that the respective bargaining powers of trade unions and employers will depend on whether trade is good or bad. Unions will obtain higher wages in times of boom; in times of slump the most they can hope for is to prevent wages from actually falling.

Where there is oligopoly or monopoly, the scope for trade-union action to raise wages will be greater. Profits will rarely have been reduced to the normal level by competition. Nor will business men have been particularly careful to avoid antagonising customers. Wages can therefore often be raised merely at the expense of profits. In oligopoly, for instance, the 'stickiness' of prices, once fixed, may mean that an oligopolist is prepared to 'absorb' moderate increases in his wage bill rather than risk being the only firm to raise prices. Again, in monopoly, the fear of antagonising public opinion may lead the monopolist to allow a trade union to encroach on his profits, and yet make him afraid of raising prices. On the other hand, of course, one of the greatest dangers that could arise would be where a strong trade union and a powerful monopolist with an inelastic demand for his product combined to exploit the public. The monopolist could afford to give higher wages because he could recoup himself by charging higher prices to his customers. With an inelastic demand for his product, such a monopolist could raise prices very considerably without causing any significant decline in the amount of his output that was bought. Hence the number of workers employed by the monopoly would be little affected by the rise in the price of the monopolist's good.

In general, however, trade unions will be unable to increase wages in any industry very far without reducing the level of employment amongst their members. An increase in wages will normally depend on an increase in the general productivity of the industry; it is at this point that the best interests of workers, employers, and the community as a whole will coincide. All will benefit from increasing productivity.

Two general points remain. First, we have discussed particular jobs purely in terms of the wages which they offer. We have implied that workers will tend to move out of an industry with low money wages and into one with high money wages. In general, this is likely to happen; but it would be both wrong and unfair to suggest that money wage rates alone attract and repel workers from particular industries. Workers will take account of many other factors. Where working conditions are good, they will not be so anxious for higher wages; where conditions are bad, 'dirt' or 'danger' money will be demanded. Similarly, if a job offers secure and stable employment a man will accept a lower weekly wage rate than if it is insecure and uncertain. In other words, the attractiveness of a job will depend not on its money rewards only, but on the 'net advantages' which it offers. Competition between workers will equalise not the wages in jobs requiring similar grades of labour, but the total 'net advantages' of these jobs.

This leads to our final point. What is the effect on wages if demand and supply conditions for labour change? The answer emerges fairly clearly from our discussion. Wages will rise in any industry if the demand for labour increases. This can happen either because labour's physical productivity rises, through increasing skill or better machines for it to use; or it can come because the price of a particular product rises as compared with the prices of other products. As we have seen, prosperity for any industry means high wages for its workers. Similarly, wages in any industry will rise if the supply of labour to it declines. Conversely, a fall in the demand for the product of a given industry; a fall in the productivity of labour in the industry; or a rise in the total number of workers seeking jobs in it will reduce the level of wages. The 'laws of supply and demand' explain the reasons for changes in the wage rates paid by any individual industry.

CHAPTER VI

PROFIT AND RENT

WE turn from the wages of labour to the profits of enterprise. Economists are agreed that 'enterprise' is the special quality which the business-man contributes to his firm, and for which he earns 'profit'. The owner of a one-man firm will supply both his capital and his own supervising labour to the firm, as well as providing 'enterprise'. His total earnings will therefore include payments on all these counts. If one takes his total earnings —what he himself calls net profits—these will comprise, first, a large payment, which represents his 'wages of management', and is equal in amount to what he would have received as a salaried manager in a similar firm. The remainder of the business-man's net profits will include a payment for the use of his capital by the firm—a return similar to that which he would have got had he invested his money in securities. If this interest payment, made to the business-man in his rôle of capitalist, is also deducted from his net profits, the residual amount is 'pure' or 'economic' profits. These represent a return to the business-man as such. A hired manager could have supplied managerial labour and could have been paid a wage. Similarly, capital could have been borrowed on payment of interest. But the business man alone can fulfil his one essential function. He alone can provide enterprise; he alone earns profit.

What, then, is this thing called enterprise? What is the essential function of the business-man in the modern economy? Economists are agreed that to provide 'enterprise' means that one takes what are known as *uninsurable risks*. Every business-man faces many different kinds of risk as he directs his firm in a world where no one can be certain what the future will bring. His plant may be burned down or burgled; he himself may die; a cargo he has paid for may go down in an accident at sea. All these are risks which men have learned to insure against. The modern economy provides insurance companies—themselves run as ordinary profit-making businesses—which allow anyone to insure against theft, death, fire and so on, merely on paying the appropriate premium.

The reason why such risks are 'insurable' is that an insurance company's statisticians will be able to tell it within close margins of error what is the probability of, say, a man of 40 dying before he reaches the age of 65. They can, similarly, say how likely it is that fires will break out in the firms of clients during any given year. Armed with such knowledge, the insurance company is able to insure people against all these risks on payment of premiums which, since they are spread among all the firm's clients, are quite low. The business-man is only too glad to pay the premium and so avoid the risk; insurance premiums represent a perfectly normal cost of production.

There is, however, one type of business risk which is so patently incalculable that no insurance company will offer to insure against it—except perhaps, at a prohibitive premium. This is the crucial risk; that the business-man may misjudge market conditions so badly that he loses money. This risk is particularly great where the product is new and untried; but it still exists where the product has sold successfully for many years. No one can be certain that even the most successful product will succeed for ever. Whilst it is not usually very difficult to guess what the costs of any product will be in the near future, it is rarely very easy to guess what demand conditions will be like. For example, one year out of ten, bad summer weather may ruin the sales of the clothing trade. But no one can tell when that year will be, or how much money will be lost because of it. It is therefore no accident that business-men cannot insure against commercial loss. There is no way for even the most brilliant statistician to say how much, if anything, either a given firm or a particular industry will lose in any given year. An insurance company which set out to insure firms against loss might well go bankrupt itself.

Here then we meet the essential function of the business-man. He is able to earn profits because he takes risks which are not easy to take and which he cannot shift to his workers, his bankers, or anyone else. He alone will lose money if he makes wrong decisions about which products to make; how big an output of each to make; what prices to charge, and so on. It is because there is always this risk of loss that, on average, business-men must earn a certain amount of 'pure' profit. Only if they can be sure of doing this will the responsibility of perpetual risk-taking seem worth while. A business-man can, after all, sell his firm, work as a hired manager, avoid taking risks, and still earn his 'wages' of management.

There will be some exceptions to this general rule. The small shopkeeper, for example, may value independence more than riches. Thus it seems likely that some owners of small shops earn *less* than they could have earned as salaried managers working for, say, a chain store. In other words, their profits are *negative*; they represent a deduction from the wages of management which the shopkeeper could have earned as an employee in a different firm. Again, it is thought that in the clothing industry, where there are many Jews who traditionally have a strong desire to be their own masters, such business-men earn less than they would get as skilled employees in other firms. Here again it seems that business-men are willing to *pay* for the privilege of independence; the profits they earn are *negative*.

This, then, is the nature of the 'enterprise'. The economy must pay 'profits' to its business-men if such enterprise is to be forthcoming. It follows that profits will depend on the supply and demand for 'enterprise'. Where many people are willing and ready to take business risks, profits will be low: where few people are willing to take the risk of becoming business-men, high profits will be earned by those who do.

This analysis has been in terms of the profits of the owner of the one-man business. How can we apply the analysis to the joint-stock company which is so typical of the twentieth century? In principle, the answer is a simple one. The 'risks of enterprise' are now borne by the ordinary shareholders of the joint-stock firm. It is they who gain if the right decisions are taken; it is they who lose if mistakes are made. Obviously, however, the whole body of ordinary shareholders in a firm cannot themselves take business decisions. They are forced to delegate such decisions to the Board of Directors and to the company's executives. Thus, the modern joint-stock company is typified by a divorce between ownership and control. The ordinary shareholder is the man who supplies 'risk capital' and who receives what profits there are. But the business decisions in his firm are taken by his appointed representatives, the directors of the company.

The economist's general explanation of the rewards of all other factors of production is similar to those for the returns to business ability and to manual labour. For example, where the supply of land available for shops and offices is small, as in the West End of London, and yet the demand for land is great, because of the high incomes to be earned there, ground-rents will be high. Similarly, when the demand for the product of a particular type of machine runs far ahead of supply, the business man who is lucky enough to own some of these machines will make a fortune. But if the demand for the product of that machine slumps, and there are nevertheless many such machines already working in factories, the returns to these machines will be so low as barely to cover their running costs.

The general rule, then, is a simple one. The price of all factors of production, men, machines, capital or enterprise, will depend on demand and supply. There will, however, be significant differences between the supply conditions for the various factors of production. The supply of labour, as we have seen, depends on sociological factors like the desire for leisure and the existence of trade unions. The supply conditions for capital goods, machines for instance, will depend partly on production conditions in the industries making them. They will also depend on the rate of interest at which money can be borrowed by businessmen who wish to buy such capital assets.

The supply of land displays interesting features of its own. Here, more than with any other factor of production, the determining feature is the scarcity of land in an absolute sense. In a city centre, for example, land is so obviously 'scarce' that one need not hesitate in ascribing the high urban ground-rents mainly to the scarcity of land. But land is scarce in a much wider sense than this. The market gardens which supply any of our towns with fruit and vegetables cannot be spaced over an unlimited area. Costs of transport mean that the market gardener wishing to supply any given town has only a limited area within which he can profitably find a site. Only if the price of vegetables rises can he afford to pay the higher transport costs which arise as he moves farther away from the town. Such a rise in prices will lead to an increase in the ground-rents which have to be paid by the fortunate market gardeners who have the 'scarce' sites near the town. Since they are on better situated land, they can afford to pay higher rents than the man who spends so much on transport to the market. Competition will therefore ensure that, in the long run, they *do* pay higher rents.

Similarly, since good agricultural land in any country is limited in amount, the best land is used first. Only if agricultural prices rise, will farming be carried out more extensively by bringing into use 'marginal land' whose cultivation had not previously paid. And as rising farm prices lead to the cultivation of progressively less and less fertile land, ground-rents on the better land will tend to rise. All farmers can sell their produce at the same competitive prices. So, those who farm the best land will earn the largest sums of money. Competition will ensure that any such extra earnings, which are due *solely* to the superior fertility of a particular farm, go, in the long run, to the landlord in the shape of higher ground-rents.

The supply conditions for the various factors of production therefore differ considerably. There are not the same differences between the forces determining the demand for the various factors of production. In all cases the demand for a factor of production will depend on its 'productivity'. This productivity, in its turn, will depend in part on the physical output which the factor of production helps to produce for its owner, and in part on the prices at which this physical output can be sold. For example, the demand for, and hence the returns to, any machine will increase if improvements are made in its physical construction. Similarly, the demand for factory sites will rise if there is a world-wide increase in the prices of industrial goods; a rise in the prices of farm products will raise the demand for, and the rents of, agricultural land.

Our study of wages has already shown us that there is a definite lower limit to the wage that labour must receive. Any individual industry has to pay its workers a wage which is high enough to prevent them leaving it and going to work in another industry. For instance, if the minimum wage paid to unskilled workers in the aircraft industry is £6 a week, unskilled workers in the automobile industry can hardly be expected to work for, say, £2 a week. They would obviously transfer themselves to the aircraft industry. A similar state of affairs exists for the economy as a whole. As we saw earlier, the minimum wage offered to labour must be at least equal to what they get 'on the dole'. If workers were paid less than this, they would almost certainly prefer to be unemployed rather than to work.

It follows that any industry must pay a certain minimum wage, slightly higher than that which a worker could receive in other jobs, to ensure that the worker does not 'transfer' his labour to another industry. This minimum wage payment is known as the worker's 'transfer earnings'. It is the amount of money which he could obtain if he were to go to work in the next most lucrative job open to him.

Now it is obvious that it is not only the industrial worker who will have to receive an income at least equal to his 'transfer earnings' if he is to stay in his present job. A factory manager may be able to earn £48 a month if he leaves his present industry and goes to work in the most lucrative job open to him in any other industry. His firm must therefore pay him at least £48 a month if he is not to leave the industry and take a job elsewhere. This £48 a month represents the manager's 'transfer earnings' and is a cost to his present industry—the cost of keeping him from moving to a different occupation.

All factors of production will have their 'transfer earnings'. Land used by a given agricultural 'industry', say, wheat farming, must be paid rent at least large enough to prevent it 'transferring' to potato-growing. Again, business men must be able to earn sufficient profits to prevent them from 'transferring' to other industries, or even selling up their firms altogether and 'relapsing into the ranks of the workers'.

It will, however, be unusual for any factor of production to earn just its transfer earnings—and nothing more. The workings of supply and demand will usually result in a price for any factor of production that is higher than the minimum reward that would be required just to keep it in the given industry. For example, a works manager who could earn only £48 a month in engineering, may be sufficiently able to earn as much as £160 a month as a mill manager in the cotton industry. Of this £160, only £48 represents the 'transfer earnings' required to keep this man in the cotton industry; the remaining £92 is a 'surplus' which he receives on account of his own innate ability, ability that is 'scarce' in the sense that few people possess it. This 'surplus', this difference between a man's income and his 'transfer earnings', is known as 'rent'; in this case a 'rent of ability'. In some ways, it is unfortunate that the word 'rent' is used in this sense. For in everyday language, a rent is a payment for the hire of a house or a flat, including interest on the landlord's capital, and need not represent any kind of 'surplus'. It must always be remembered, therefore, that the economist uses 'rent' in this particular and special sense of the difference between what a factor of production *does* earn in any given industry and what it *must* earn to prevent it from leaving that industry and going to work elsewhere.

Rents will be earned wherever all units of a particular factor of production are not of equal efficiency or ability. For example, as we have seen, land is of unequal fertility. Some areas of land are more productive than others, and the rents that the better farms yield will be higher than rents on less fertile land. It is only 'marginal' land, which is only just worth farming, that will earn no 'rent' at all. High rents are a reward to the high fertility or the great ability of particular units of a factor of production.

High rents are nevertheless an indication not of the bounty of nature in producing many men of high ability; they are rather a sign of her niggardliness in producing so few of them. For if all men were of equally great ability, competition would force their incomes down to the level of their transfer earnings; no 'rent of ability' would be earned. Similarly, high rents for the best farm land result from the fact that good agricultural land, and hence agricultural produce as a whole, is not unlimited in amount. The fertility of land is not high enough for people to be able to satisfy all their needs for food from the best land. Thus even poor land can earn a moderate rent in addition to its 'transfer earnings'; and the best land can earn a very high rent.

There may, however, be a quite different reason for the high 'rents' earned by, say, some skilled workers and some business-men. As we have seen already, some skilled workers may deliberately restrict entry into their own particular trades in order to earn abnormally high wages—wages considerably in excess of 'transfer earnings'. Part of these high wages may represent a 'rent of ability' paid because workers possess great ability in their trade; but another part of these wages will be a 'rent of monopoly'. It will be earned because the workers in the trade have restricted entry into it, and thereby obtained a 'monopoly' of their particular type of labour. It is often suggested that this has been one result, perhaps unintended, of apprenticeship regulations governing entry into the ranks of the compositors in the British printing trade.

Even more likely is the case where a business-man possesses some 'monopoly power', great or small. The monopolist, in the strict sense of that term, is likely to earn more than the 'transfer earnings' which the task of 'risk-taking' alone would enable him to earn. The fact that he has no rivals means that he can earn a 'monopoly rent' by charging relatively high prices for his output. It follows that one should be careful to distinguish in one's own mind between profits earned by taking commercial risks, and profits originating in a business-man's monopolistic control over his own section of the industry. Nor, of course, will such 'monopoly rents' be earned only by the true monopolist. A group of oligopolists, since they represent only a relatively small number of firms in what may be a large market, may earn 'monopoly rent' by making a quasi-monopolistic agreement between themselves. And even in a competitive industry, provided that each firm is able to produce its own individual 'differentiated' product, small 'monopoly rents' may be earned because, temporarily, given firms have managed to steal a march on their competitors, and can charge a high price for a 'novelty' product. This last type of 'monopoly rent' is, of course, likely to be transitory. Competition from rivals will soon eliminate it.

We deal, finally, with an interesting type of 'rent'—that earned by machines. In the case of both land and human beings, there is little or nothing which can be done to improve their innate fertility or ability, as the case may be. It is true that land can be fertilised and men educated; but unless the land or the men possess the right inherent qualities, there is little likelihood of either earning high rents. In the case of capital goods, for example, machines, the position is quite the opposite. If there is a shortage of machinery, and the existing machines earn exceptionally high returns, there is no reason why these high earnings should persist. For the number of machines in existence depends on human decisions, and that number can be increased or decreased quite deliberately in a way that the innate ability of man or the fertility of land cannot.

Let us assume that there is a sudden and permanent increase in the demand for a particular product. Its price will rise. This will automatically raise the earnings of the machines which make that product. The number of these machines is likely to have been adjusted initially to the previous level of demand. There will be sufficiently few of them for the new, higher, level of demand to enable them to yield a high return to the owners of the machines. In the short run, these high returns may persist. In the long run, however, more machines will be made and used, so that the return on each of these machines will tend to become equal to the long-run cost of keeping it in existence. Much of this long-run cost is likely to take the form of interest charges on the capital sunk in the machine.

In the short run, then, a machine can earn a kind of 'rent', in the shape of a return which is bigger than what is needed to keep the machine in existence. But this abnormally high return is not a real rent. No true rent can disappear in the long run merely because the high rent itself causes an increase in the supply of the factor of production. No increase in the supply of a factor that is earning a true rent can take place *as a direct result* of the high returns being earned by it. High rents of land, resulting from high agricultural prices, cannot increase the total supply of land in acountry. These high rents can therefore persist over a long period of time, and can only disappear if the prices of agricultural products fall. High returns from machines *will* increase the long-run supply of machines and this increase in the supply of machines will eliminate the abnormally high returns which they have been earning.

CHAPTER VII

MONEY AND INTEREST

WE have so far shown how the prices of goods and factors of production are determined in particular industries. Our next main task is to explain how the general level of prices, and of returns to factors of production, is determined. Even more important, we must discover the factors on which the general level of employment and activity in a community depend. The twentieth century has been one in which both unemployment and also over-employment and inflation have been widely experienced. Economists have, since 1930, devoted much of their energy to explaining these phenomena and we shall summarise their current views in the following few chapters. This chapter deals with two factors which are extremely important in helping to determine the level of economic activity—the money supply and the rate of interest.

The rate of interest is the 'price' at which money can be borrowed, just as wages are the 'price' at which labour can be hired. It is expressed as a rate per cent per annum, for the obvious reason that money is borrowed for considerable periods of time, and a rate per cent is therefore the most convenient way of reckoning its cost. There is no need to spend time in discovering what money is. Everyone knows. It is important to realise, however, that in a country like modern Britain, the greater part of its money does not take the form of bank notes and coin; most of it is the 'bank credit' which people and firms hold in their bank accounts. The precise form of money is perhaps less important, economically, than the functions that it fulfils. For the economist regards anything which performs these functions as money.

Money fulfils two main purposes. First, and most important, it acts as a 'medium of exchange'. People accept money in exchange for work or for commodities because they know that they, in turn, will be able to obtain goods and services from other people in exchange for this money. Money must therefore possess the basic attribute of being 'generally acceptable'. Only if everyone is prepared to accept it can money be relied upon to act as the medium of exchange in a country. This explains why so much emphasis is always laid on maintaining 'confidence' in the currency. If such confidence ceases, as in times of very rapid inflation, people will not hold money, even for a few hours, for fear that it will lose much of its value.

The second main function of money is to act as a 'store of value'. It is usually both unsatisfactory and impracticable to try to preserve one's wealth over periods of years by storing up commodities. Money is much simpler to keep safely. It is, however, most important in this instance that money should not vary greatly in value. Even in inflation money can often continue to serve as a medium of exchange, since it is possible to spend one's income immediately upon receiving it. But one will not store money over periods of years without being reasonably confident that it is likely to preserve its value. It is for this reason that most modern governments regard it as one of their primary responsibilities to maintain the purchasing power of money.

Lastly, money performs the further functions of acting as the unit of account in which both current purchases of goods, and deferred repayments of loans, are calculated. That these further functions need not necessarily be fulfilled by the same kind of money as the first two is shown by the fact that prices in Britain are often calculated in 'guineas', though no such coin now exists.

The rate of interest, we have said, is the 'price' of money loans—the price at which money is lent and borrowed. Alternatively, it can be defined as the price of present money in terms of pieces of paper promising to pay given amounts of money, on specified terms, in the future. It is the price of money in terms of 'bonds', which have specified repayment dates, specified conditions for making interest payments and definite rates of interest to be paid on them. Such, for example, are the bonds issued by Governments.

The question now is : what determines whether the rate of interest is high or low, for example 3 or 6 per cent per annum, under various circumstances? This is an important question. During the first half of the twentieth century the rate of interest on long-term British Government stock, for instance the undated 'Old Consols', has fluctuated to almost the full extent of these rather wide limits.

Most economists think nowadays that the rate of interest, at least in the short run, is mainly determined by 'monetary forces'. By this they mean that on the one hand it depends on the actions of the monetary authorities—the Central Bank and the Government. On the other hand, they think that it depends on the attitude of individuals and businesses towards holding money as an alternative to holding bonds. The Central Bank controls the supply, or stock, of money; and the terms on which individuals are prepared to hold this stock of money can be regarded as the demand for it.

These words, the demand for and supply of money, are not in everyday use; they are not even part of the technical vocabulary of business-men and bankers. They therefore need further explanation. Both in ordinary language and, for example, in the City of London's 'Money Market', the word money is used in the sense of money to borrow and not money to hold. This everyday use of the word 'money' is sensible and has many advantages. The trouble with using it for our purposes is that if one defined the demand for money as the demand to borrow money, one would then have to distinguish the various, very different purposes to which the money was to be put after being borrowed.

For example, a business-man may borrow money by obtaining an advance from his banker, merely in order to increase the amount of money in his bank account. On the other hand, the same business-man may borrow money to be spent immediately on buying a machine. In this second case it is not the money which he really wants. His increased demand is for machinery, not for money. In the first case, however, it was for money and for nothing else that his demand had increased. To avoid ambiguity economists therefore call the demand for money in the first sense the 'demand for money to hold'.

The main assumption of present-day economics is that, if one considers the demand for money, the typical choice, for both individuals and firms, is not nowadays between money and goods, but between money and bonds. As we have seen, it is not practicable to store one's wealth in the form of commodities. The only real alternative to holding wealth in the form of money is not the purchase of goods; it is the purchase of either Government securities or securities issued by industrial companies. When people become more anxious to hold money in the form of cash instead of holding securities, the rate of interest will have to rise in order to persuade the community to hold the same total amount of securities as before.

The rate of interest, then, is the reward offered to people to induce them to hold securities instead of cash. For cash is 'safe' in the sense that there is no danger of physical deterioration or capital loss. Securities can and do vary in value. It is because of this risk that a capital loss may be incurred when one purchases securities, that interest payments have to be made to induce people to hold securities instead of hoarding money.

The demand for money to hold, or *liquidity preference* as it is called, depends on three 'motives for liquidity'—on three main reasons why people and institutions prefer to hold a 'liquid' asset like money instead of, say, Government securities or shares of industrial companies.

The first of these motives is known as the 'transactions motive'. Both individuals and businesses will need 'ready cash' always on hand. Individuals will need it because they will receive their incomes only once per week or per month, whilst they will need to make some payments, say to shopkeepers, on most days in the week or the month. Businesses will need always to hold some money in order to pay bills from suppliers, to pay wages, and so on. One can reasonably assume that the total amount of money in a country held under this transactions motive will depend almost entirely on the level of individual incomes. The richer a man or a firm is the more money he will have *on average* in his bank account; and the nation's money holdings will be the sum of such individual stores.

Second, money will be held to satisfy the 'precautionary motive', to provide for a 'rainy day'. Individuals will wish to provide against unemployment or accident; firms will wish to prepare for the danger that trade conditions may turn against them and they may be forced for a time to 'live on their fat'. The amount of money held under the precautionary motive will depend mainly on the size of the community's income. As people become better off, they will feel able to set more of their wealth aside, to provide against the uncertainties of the future.

Third, money will be held to satisfy the 'speculative motive'. It is here that the rate of interest itself becomes an important factor determining the demand for money. As we have seen, liquidity preference under the transactions and precautionary motives depends mainly on the level of people's income. Given the level of incomes, therefore, the demand for money cannot alter because of changes in these two motives—unless people's

F

habits change. But changes in the amount of money demanded can still occur, if the rate of interest varies.

At any time people will regard one rate of interest as normal. For example, in Britain today a rate of interest on long-term Government securities of 1 per cent would be regarded as phenomenally low, and one of 7 per cent as abnormally high. The lower the rate of interest at any time happens to be, the more confident everyone will be that it will rise again in the near future, and vice versa.

Now the rate of interest is inversely related to the prices of 'bonds'. As we have seen, these are securities which give a fixed annual yield, say 4 per cent, during the whole period of their life. Thus, for example, a bond may be issued at a price of £100 when the rate of interest is 4 per cent. If the rate of interest now falls to 2 per cent, the price of this bond will rise to £200. For purchasers of bonds will now be completely indifferent whether they buy new bonds for £100 with interest of £2 per annum, or whether they buy an existing bond which yields a nominal return of £4 per annum—but pay £200 for it. For in this case too the rate of interest they actually receive will be 2 per cent. Thus, a fall in the rate of interest will mean exactly the same thing as a rise in bond prices; a rise in the rate of interest represents a fall in bond prices. For example, if the rate of interest rises to 8 per cent, the price on the Stock Exchange of our 4 per cent £100 bond, issued at par, will now fall to £50.

When the rate of interest is considered to be 'low' compared with its 'normal' level, it follows that most people will confidently expect a rise in the near future. Since this rise, when it comes, means a reduction in the price of Stock Exchange securities, there will be no point in buying such securities now. One should clearly wait until after the expected rise in the rate of interest has occurred. With a 'low' rate of interest, therefore, people will prefer to hold money rather than bonds. They will hope to use their money to buy bonds at 'bargain prices' after the rate of interest has risen. Similarly, if the rate of interest is high, people will wish to hold securities rather than money. Since the rate of interest is high, people will expect it to fall in the near future; they will expect bond prices to rise. It will therefore seem desirable to buy bonds whilst the rate of interest is high, and their price is low, in order, perhaps, to sell at a profit later on.

Therefore, a valid generalisation is possible. The lower the rate of interest, the greater will be the demand for money to hold under the speculative motive. For the lower the rate of interest is, the more certain people will be that it will rise in the future. At the same time, the lower will be the return that they will be offered as a reward for risking such a capital loss if they buy bonds. Liquidity preference under the speculative motive will increase steadily as the rate of interest falls.

The demand for money, then, will depend partly on the level of the community's income and partly on the rate of interest. We now consider the factors which determine the supply of money.

The money supply in the modern community is under the ultimate control of the Central Bank and hence, usually, of the Government. For the Central Bank is the Government's bank and will hold accounts of, and also issue instructions to, the ordinary commercial banks. The Central Bank will issue all bank notes ; and the volume of bank deposits which commercial banks will be willing to issue will depend, through compulsion or convention, on the amount of 'cash'—mainly bank notes—which the commercial banks hold. In Britain, for example, bankers found during the nineteenth century that it was only possible to maintain public confidence in their solvency if they kept some 10 per cent of their total deposits in the form of Bank of England notes. Otherwise, people would find that not all demands for bank notes could be met, and they would rush to convert their bank deposits into bank notes—there would be a 'run' on the bank in question. The fact that, even if the banker acted prudently and 'backed' 10 per cent of his deposits with bank notes, he could never issue bank notes in exchange for *all* his customers' deposits on demand did not matter. So long as the '10 per cent rule' was adhered to there was no danger of any customer being unable to obtain 'cash' whenever he wanted it. All clients were quite content and the 'solvency' of the bank was preserved.

The need to keep a certain ratio between their 'cash' and their total deposits remains the essence of sound banking policy. In Britain, for instance, all commercial banks now keep 8 per cent of their total deposits in the form of 'cash'—either actual bank notes or, equally good, deposits in an account with the Bank of England, which can be turned into bank notes at any time. This 8 per cent cash/deposit ratio is strictly observed by all British banks.

It follows from this that the Government, through the Central Bank, can exercise fairly complete control over the supply of money. If the Government wishes to increase the money supply, it will instruct the Bank of England to buy securities. Then, an agent of the Central Bank known as the 'Special Buyer' will purchase short-term securities from banks or from members of the short-term money market in London. Alternatively, or in addition, the 'Government Broker' will purchase long-term securities on the Stock Exchange. Such purchases (or sales) of securities by the Central Bank are called 'open market operations'. The securities in question will be paid for by the Bank of England, with drafts on itself which will find their way into the hands of the commercial banks and will thereby augment their deposits with the Bank of England. This increase in the commercial banks' 'cash' will, in turn, enable them to increase the amount of their loans to the Government, to nationalised or private industry and to individuals.

But it follows from the existence of the 8 per cent cash/deposit ratio that the commercial banks will be able to expand their advances to customers by several times the amount which the Government, through the Central Bank, has spent on open-market operations. On the face of it, if each commercial bank keeps only 8 per cent of its deposits in the form of cash, an increase of £100 in its account with the Central Bank should allow it to increase its total loans by £1250—by $12\frac{1}{2}$ times the cash acquired. In practice the multiple is not $12\frac{1}{2}$, but perhaps 3 or 4. For when any commercial bank increases its loans, some of the cash which it has acquired through open-market operations will be lost. It will go to business men, shopkeepers and work-people. It is thought, therefore, that in modern Britain a given expenditure on open-market operations would probably lead to a total increase in the country's money supply of about three times that amount.

Conversely, of course, if the Central Bank, through its agents, *sells* Government long- or short-term securities, there will be a multiple *reduction* in the country's money supply.

Having seen what determines the demand and the supply conditions for money, we can now see how, between them, these demands and supplies determine the rate of interest. Let us consider how the banking authorities can raise or lower the rate of interest in accordance with the needs of the moment—how they can make money 'dear' or 'cheap'.

To lower the rate of interest, as to lower any price, it will be necessary to increase the supply of money, to reduce the demand for money—or both. In practice, it is often simpler to operate on the money supply. Since the demand for money depends so largely on psychology and convention, it is hard to make changes of the right degree, and in the right direction. Nevertheless, it is not impossible to reduce the amount of money which the community will demand at any given rate of interest—even though it may not be easy. One weapon which can be used to do this in Britain is 'Bank Rate'. Technically, this is the rate of interest at which institutions in the City of London can borrow from the Bank of England. It is a 'penal' rate; and therefore the 'City' institutions in question only borrow from the Bank of England when money is extremely 'tight'. The Bank of England is 'the lender of last resort'.

However, economists are agreed that, in practice, Bank Rate today largely represents a 'danger' or 'fair weather' signal to the economy as a whole. If Bank Rate falls, people will revise their ideas of what is a 'normal' rate of interest in a downward direction. If it rises, they will do the opposite. This is partly because by convention 'the City' always follows the Government's lead and alters the rate of interest on many kinds of loan in the appropriate direction; and partly because there will always be the knowledge that the Government will be prepared to embark on more direct and effective measures to lower or raise interest rates if this is necessary.

If the rather 'technical' device of Bank Rate is spurned, as it was by the Labour Government between 1945 and 1951, it may still be possible to 'talk' the rate of interest up or down. To lower the rate of interest, for example, Government spokesmen can attempt to convince the business community that 'cheap money' is coming to stay. If such measures succeed, people will come to look upon a lower rate of interest as 'normal'. As a result, liquidity preference at each rate of interest will diminish —the demand for money at the current rate of interest will decline, and, given the supply of money, the rate of interest will fall.

But when a cheap money policy is being pursued, the supply of money will not normally be given; it will usually be increased by means of open-market operations, thereby reinforcing the Government's attempt to reduce the demand for money. The Central Bank will purchase securities and will thus expand the supply of money. This procedure will have an important feature. By operating through the Stock Exchange, as well as in the short-term money market, and thus increasing the demand for securities whilst leaving their supply unaffected, the open-market operations will automatically lower the rate of interest in an important part of the market.

The Government therefore has considerable control over the rate of interest; but this control can never be quite complete in a field where psychological factors are so important. For example, it appears to be impossible to drive down the long-term rate of interest below, say, 2 per cent. At this level liquidity preference becomes infinite; however much money is pumped into the system it will all be held by someone. People will have become so convinced that a further reduction in the rate of interest is out of the question, that they will not be prepared to use any of the newly created money to buy securities. They will hold all of it in the form of cash. Perhaps the correct evaluation of the position, then, is to say that the Government has very consider-able control over the rate of interest, *especially* when the Government and the public are agreed about the kind of policy to be followed.

All that has been said above applies, in the opposite direction, to a rise in the rate of interest. If the Government wishes to raise the rate of interest, to make money 'dear', it must increase the demand for money and reduce the supply. The demand for money can be increased if people are persuaded that the 'normal' rate of interest has now become higher than previously. This can be done either by raising 'Bank Rate' as a signal that market rates of interest should rise; or by 'talking up' the rate of interest. Such measures will have some effect, but they will normally need to be reinforced by open-market operations. The sale of long- and short-term securities by the Central Bank will, on the one hand, reduce the 'cash' resources of the commercial banks and, on the other, lower security prices—raise interest rates—on the Stock Exchange. One suspects that an increase in the rate of interest will be easier to achieve than a fall. For it is always easier to make people afraid that share prices will fall than to convince them that share prices are on the point of rising. It is easier to make people pessimistic than to make them optimistic.

This analysis has been carried out entirely in terms of a deliberate Government decision to change interest rates. Changes in these rates can, of course, occur also as the result of spontaneous changes in the demand for money; and the analysis outlined above can easily allow for such changes. A spontaneous increase in the demand for money, given the supply of money, will raise the rate of interest, and vice versa. However, in the modern world, it is much more likely that any significant change in the rate of interest will result from deliberate action by Governments rather than from spontaneous changes in any country's demand for money.

Finally, two qualifications must be made to the above analysis. First, we have discussed open-market operations solely in terms of their effect on bond prices and the rates of interest that bonds offer. But there will also be many *equities*[1] which are bought and sold on the Stock Exchange. The annual dividend yields on equities varies according to the financial and economic position of the borrowers; it is not fixed in advance as is the rate of interest on bonds. Our procedure was legitimate, because a Central Bank will not normally carry out open-market purchases of industrial equities and debentures[2]—only Government bonds. But the effect of the open-market operations will spread to other securities and the price of equities will change to some extent in sympathy with the price of bonds. For bonds and equities will be regarded as fairly good substitutes for each other by investors.

Our second qualification is that we have so far followed the usual convention of talking of *the* rate of interest. In practice, there will be a whole complex of rates of interest. Nevertheless, all these rates, long and short, high and low, will be associated, and will move upwards and downwards in concert. Differences between interest rates will depend mainly on the differing lengths of the period of the loan, and on the differing degrees of risk associated with the firms issuing securities. Because of the smaller risk that interest payments—or the repayment of the loan—will go by default, the British Government can borrow more cheaply than the average industrial company can when it issues debentures. The latter can, in turn, borrow more cheaply than those financing a highly risky gamble. Similarly, a short-term loan will be obtained more cheaply than a long-term one.

---

[1] Equities are securities paying an annual dividend yield whose amount varies according to the prosperity of the firm issuing them. An ordinary share of an industrial company is therefore an equity.

[2] A debenture, like a bond, carries a fixed rate of return per annum. But debentures are issued by industry and bonds by Governments.

There is less danger that the investor will need to sell out at a loss if interest rates rise before the security matures. All these differing rates of interest will bear a fairly definite relationship to each other. All will be high together and all will be low together, according to the general policy of the Government.

CHAPTER VIII

THE LEVEL OF ECONOMIC ACTIVITY

In this chapter we shall show what factors determine the level of activity in a country at any given moment. In the following chapter we shall show how this level of activity can vary over time, and, in particular, the problems which arise when there is unemployment on the one hand, or inflation on the other.

The first point to note is that the same basic factors will determine the level of economic activity, the level of employment and the level of total incomes in a country. All will be high together and all will be low together. Our analysis here will be primarily in terms of national income, but it applies equally to employment and to activity in general.

The basic proposition is a simple one. The level of any nation's total income, and also its total employment, will depend on the total amount of money which is spent on the goods it produces. This total national expenditure can be split into three main parts—expenditure by consumers on consumption goods and services, expenditure on capital assets by businesses and expenditure on both consumption and capital goods by central or local governments. In order to discover what determines the level of national income, we must study these three main items of national expenditure—consumption, investment and Government expenditure.

Expenditure on consumption, both by individuals and in total by the whole community, will depend on the level of the national, and hence of individual, incomes. A high level of income will mean a high level of national consumption; a low national income will mean little expenditure on consumption goods. It does not follow, however, that consumers, either individually or in total, will spend the same *proportion* of a small income on consumption goods as they will when their income is high. It is generally agreed that at low levels of income consumers will spend almost the whole of their earnings on those goods which they regard as 'necessary' to existence. Once a certain point is reached, that point differing with personal idio-syncrasies, with social groups and with the type of society, consumers will begin to save some part of their income. They will feel that they can afford to put aside part of their earnings to provide for the future needs of either themselves or their children.

When the stage has been reached where some money is being saved, any short-run rise of income is likely to lead to larger savings and hence to the consumption of a *smaller proportion* of the increased income. In the long run, however, people will become used to their larger incomes and the proportion saved will fall—perhaps even to the original level.

It follows that a major cause of short-period changes in consumption, and therefore in savings, will be changes in the level of the national income. It does not, of course, automatically follow that this is the *only* factor affecting the level of savings. In the past economists have often emphasised a connection between the rate of interest and savings. People are uncertain about the future. For example, they have no absolute certainty how long they will remain alive. It is therefore necessary to offer people some inducement to persuade them to forgo the certain pleasures of present consumption and save their money in the less certain hope of spending it to advantage later on. Interest payments were thought by many nineteenth-century economists to provide an important inducement to people to refrain from present consumption—to save. For interest payments increase the total value of a sum of money when that money is lent out for a period of time. So, in principle, they appear to make it worth 'waiting' some time to enjoy the pleasures of consumption. This view is now treated with much scepticism. With the relatively low interest rates at present prevailing, especially in countries where taxes are high, it is felt that changes in the rate of interest have far less effect on the nation's total savings than do changes in the level of the national income.

A further difficulty is that changes in the rate of interest, if they affect savings at all, may do so in the wrong direction. A man may decide, when the rate of interest is 2 per cent, that he will save £10,000 and enjoy a retirement income of £200 a year. If the rate of interest rises to 4 per cent, however, he may decide that £200 a year is a perfectly satisfactory pension and cut his total savings to £5000. Hence a *rise* in the rate of interest might well *reduce* total savings. Such uncertainties have led to the present feeling that the level of income alone is the major factor in determining the savings of individuals and of the whole community.

The savings policies of businesses, which in turn affect the consumption expenditure of shareholders in their capacity as consumers, are equally likely to depend mainly on the level of the national income. When the national income is high, firms' gross profits will be high, and vice versa.

There is, however, no reason for supposing that the relationship between the gross profits of firms and those firms' savings will follow the same kind of pattern as with consumers. It seems probable that, with fairly small changes in the national income, firms will save a *larger* proportion of their profits when these profits are small and a smaller one when profits are high. Firms will, for instance, often put the same amount of money into their depreciation reserves and the like when trade is bad as when it is good; and this same absolute sum of money will represent a larger *proportion* of the firms' abnormally low gross profits. Similarly, when times are bad, firms may set aside money to enable them to pay at any rate a modest dividend in future years, even if trade does not improve. It follows that, provided economic fluctuations are not too great, a fall in activity may actually *raise* business savings as a proportion of business income, and perhaps even in absolute terms.

The fundamental generalisation is certain; the consumption expenditure, and consequently the savings, of any community depends mainly on the level of that community's total income. It is worth noting, here, that in post-war Britain it has been business firms which have done most of the nation's saving. The absolute amount of money saved by private individuals has been small.

We have so far made no real progress towards explaining what determines the level of income in a country, for we have merely seen that, given consumers' saving habits, the first component of national income—consumption expenditure—depends on the size of the national income itself. Investment leads a far more independent existence and is prone to cause fluctuations in the level of income and activity. The volume of investment carried out in any community at any time depends, on the one hand, on the expected returns from such investment. On the other hand, it depends on the cost of acquiring money to carry out that investment—on the rate of interest at which money to finance investment can be borrowed either privately or by, say, floating a new issue of debentures on the Stock Exchange.

First, a word of warning is necessary. By investment, economists mean the construction of any physical capital assets —factories, machinery, office buildings, harbours, etc.—which will be used to produce or transport consumption or capital goods. Investment *does not* here mean buying Stock Exchange securities, old or new, even though these securities are issued to finance actual 'bricks and mortar' investment. In other words, we distinguish between *real* and *money* investment.

Let us first consider the demand for investment goods. This depends on the returns expected from the new acts of investment. A business-man who is wondering whether to build or buy a new machine or factory will have a rough idea of the returns which he expects from this capital asset, and also of the length of the asset's useful working life. He can express these expected returns as a percentage yield per annum over that working life. For example, a machine may cost £1000 and be expected to last for ten years. The business-man may expect that, in each of these ten years, the machine will produce goods worth £100— after deducting all the payments which will have to be made to provide for the ultimate replacement of the machine itself, and to pay for the other factors of production, labour, raw materials, etc., which co-operate with the machine in producing final output. Over the ten years of its life, then, the machine will yield an annual return equal to 10 per cent of its initial cost. This 10 per cent yield represents *the rate of return over cost* of the machine.

The return on any other capital asset can be calculated in the same way, and the demand by business firms for new assets will depend on these expected rates of return. Just as the productivity of labour, in terms of the money value of the output it produces, will determine the number of workers a business man will employ, so the expected rate of return on each type of capital asset will determine the extent of the business community's investment in that asset.

Against these expected rates of return must be set the cost of borrowing money to build the assets in question—in the form of bank loans, mortgages, or the floating of new debenture issues on the Stock Exchange. We have already seen that the general rate of interest at which industrial borrowing can take place will depend on the monetary policy pursued by the Government through the Central Bank. There will, of course, be variations around this general rate. Firms in 'risky' industries will borrow less cheaply than others. Long-established and reputable firms will borrow more cheaply than those on the 'speculative fringe'. But the main factor determining whether money is 'cheap' or 'dear' to investors as a whole will be the country's general monetary policy.

We can now see the link between the rate of interest and the level of investment. The lower the rate of interest the greater the volume of investment is likely to be, and vice versa. For example, suppose that, at a given moment, the most promising investment projects in a community—those which the business community is uncertain whether it should carry out—promise an annual yield of 5 per cent. If the general rate of interest on industrial debentures is itself 6 per cent, these schemes will not appear worth while. If the debenture loan rate drops to 2 per cent, they may be carried out.

It does not necessarily follow, however, that there will be any widespread tendency to push investment in all firms and industries to the point where no investment project is left unstarted which offers a return at least as great as the rate of interest. Theoretically, this ought to happen, for business-men ought to want to maximise profits by pocketing any difference between the yields of investments and the rate of interest at which these acts of investment can be financed. In practice, there are several reasons why investment will cease to expand whilst there is still a gap between the, say, 10 per cent expected rate of return in a particular field of investment and the, say, 5 per cent rate of interest which has to be paid on industrial debentures.

First, there is probably a limit to the rate at which any firm or industry can expand, however rosy prospects for the future may seem. So, whilst a fall in the rate of interest may *increase* the number of investment schemes carried out in a given period, there will be a definite physical limit to the absolute number that can be carried out simultaneously ; and this limit may not be closely related to the schemes' apparent profitability.

Second, whilst an expected return on any asset of, say, 10 per cent may represent the best estimate of that return which the business-man can obtain, he may not put much faith in this estimate. He will therefore stop short of pushing investment to the point where expected returns exactly equal the rate of interest. For example, if a project which is just thought unprofitable promises a return of 10 per cent and the rate of interest is

6 per cent, the 4 per cent margin between the two represents the measure of the business-man's lack of confidence in his own estimate of the rate of return.

Finally, taxation problems may creep in. A complicated tax system may mean that taxation cannot be allowed for satisfactorily in making estimates of rates of return; however simple the tax system is, future tax changes cannot be accurately foreseen. Here again, therefore, the business-man may mentally discount the expected rate of return on an asset to allow for the complexity of the existing tax system and for future tax changes—though the exact nature of the discounting process may never be completely clear, even to the business-man himself.

Our general propositions about investment remain unaffected by these qualifications. First, a community will carry out a greater total amount of investment when the rate of interest is low than when it is high. Second, investment activity will be greater in those industries where rates of return are high, perhaps because of improved demand conditions or because of the development of new and more effective machines. It will be smaller in those industries where expected returns are low.

These conclusions suggest a moral for monetary policy. When it is wished to stimulate investment, the rate of interest should be lowered, and vice versa. There are, however, difficulties. First, it is possible that the volume of investment activity may respond little to a fall in the rate of interest; investment may be 'inelastic' in its response to changes in the rate of interest. Since, as we have seen, it is unlikely that the rate of interest can in any case be lowered beyond a certain minimum, say 2 per cent, reductions in the rate of interest which are sufficiently large to evoke a considerable increase in the volume of investment, and hence of employment, may not be possible. If a further increase in investment is needed, more direct measures may be essential. For example, the Government may find it necessary to undertake investment activity on its own account.

A second difficulty arising from the nature of investment decisions is that business-men's estimates of the expected rates of return on investment activity are prone to change substantially and violently when they change at all. Since no one can foresee the future, all business-men tend to place undue emphasis on those facts which are known for certain, not least the Stock Exchange quotations of the shares of companies similar to their own.

The main functions of the Stock Exchange are two. First, it enables people to buy and sell securities, so that an individual shareholder need not consider his loan to the firm in question as a permanent and immutable transaction. Second, it provides a 'new issue market' in which money may be borrowed to meet the expanding needs of existing firms or to allow new firms to be set up.

By providing a market for the exchange of existing securities, the Stock Exchange also gives the opportunity for the business community to carry out a perpetual review of the current value of shares of all kinds. In other words, it provides a good indication of how the 'mass opinion' of those who buy and sell shares currently views the prospects of the various industries in the country. The business-man who is meditating a new act of investment will inevitably give weight to the current valuation of the shares of firms similar to his own. When the shares of these firms stand at high prices, he will view his own future prospects optimistically, and vice versa. For, amid all the uncertainties of the future, the Stock Exchange valuation of the shares of firms in his own industry stands out as the one 'hard' fact.

This emphasis, in making investment decisions, on the Stock Exchange's estimate of the future has its unfortunate effects. First, the valuation is made by many people, professionals and others, all of whom are equally ignorant of the future prospects of the firms in question. Like all such manifestations of 'mass opinion', share prices are prone to fall sharply when buyers and sellers become pessimistic and to rise equally violently when they become more confident. Rises and falls in share prices therefore tend to be more exaggerated than the true facts—when they are finally known—would have warranted.

As a result, business-men's expectations of the returns from investment—and hence the volume of investment activity itself —tend to fluctuate equally violently. At various times in the past century such fluctuations in the volume of investment have led to serious fluctuations in the level of activity in individual countries and in the world as a whole; for example, the 1929 slump.

A further feature of the modern economy is that there is little point in those who make their living by buying and selling Stock Exchange securities, however omniscient, trying to make a living by evaluating correctly the long-term prospects of any given firm or industry. For, to make a living on this basis, a man may need to wait a lifetime; and far greater rewards are likely to be his if he contents himself with foreseeing the, perhaps wildly unrealistic, price at which 'mass opinion' will value the share in a few days' or weeks' time. Long-term 'investing' on the Stock Exchange is both less lucrative and more boring than pitting one's wits against those of other 'investors' in the quest for quick and enticing gains. It follows that not only will the level of investment in a country tend to fluctuate violently when the economic climate alters ; the share prices upon which investment decisions tend to be based may well bear little relation to the true facts of the situation for considerable periods of time.

Finally, an important peculiarity of investment decisions is that they depend on the *expected* and not the realised returns to the investment in question. This, of course, is not an unmixed blessing. Many factories and machines will be bought which, in the cold light of history, come nowhere near satisfying the rosy expectations of the original investor. If business men had more to rely on than their uncertain hopes and fears, such acts of investment would never have occurred. On the other hand, it is equally possible that the pessimism of individual business-men, or an inauspicious general economic situation, may stifle at birth projects that would have paid for themselves many times over. Here again, the realities of the world mean that, when conditions are good, an already high level of investment will be increased still further ; when times are bad, few people will dare to invest at all.

Having discussed consumption and investment, we turn, finally, to Government expenditure. As we have seen, Government spending, on both consumer and capital goods, will generate a further part of the national income. We shall discuss such spending in detail at a later stage. For the present we may merely note that it will normally be determined as much by political as by economic factors.

CHAPTER IX

ECONOMIC FLUCTUATIONS

IN the previous chapter we saw that the main determinant of consumption in a country is the level of the national income. It follows that there is an important relationship between consumption and investment. For a change in the volume of investment undertaken in a country will mean an automatic increase in the level of income by that amount. This initial increase in the national income will cause a consequent increase in consumption expenditure, people spending a proportion of their increased earnings on consumer goods. But the process does not stop there. The increased consumption expenditure will occur because both workers and employers in the investment goods industries spend the extra money, which they receive as a result of the community's increased investment expenditure, on buying consumer goods. In so doing, these workers will pass on their increased incomes to other people, perhaps shopkeepers. The shopkeepers in their turn will spend at least part of their extra receipts on consumption goods; the process is cumulative.

A given increase in the volume of investment activity in any community will therefore give rise to an increase in income which is several times as large. This is known as a 'multiplier process'. The 'multiplier' itself tells us by how many times the total increase in national income exceeds the increase in investment expenditure which gave rise to it.

To show how the multiplier works, let us assume that a given economy has been operating for a considerable period of time at a given, fairly low, level of income and activity, with no significant economic fluctuations. An increase in investment activity now takes place, because the Government, worried about the low level of employment in the country, wishes to take steps to raise incomes and reduce unemployment. We assume that this is not a mere once-for-all act of investment, but that the Government undertakes to carry out the new, increased volume of investment in each succeeding year—or whatever period of time is most convenient. Finally, we suppose that the process is allowed to work itself out completely, all other things remaining equal. Government expenditure rises by just the planned amount and is constant at its new level; non-government investment remains completely unaltered; and the only changes in consumption spending are those which result from the multiplier effects of the initial change in investment.

In these relatively simple circumstances, the working of the multiplier can be easily explained. Since the original level of income was abnormally low, there will be no physical obstacles, like shortage of machinery, factory space or labour, preventing a rise in output. An increase in income can therefore take place quite easily, without causing any marked rise in the general price level. So, once the Government 'public works' investment scheme is undertaken, the level of national income will begin to rise. It will continue to rise for some time, as the increased incomes resulting from the increase in Government investment activity are passed on through the spending of successive recipients. But gradually the initial impetus will be lost. The rate at which income is rising will slow down, and the economy will finally settle down to stability at a new and higher level of income. The difference between the 'pre-public works' income and the final income will be a certain multiple of the amount of the extra Government spending on the public works schemes This multiple is the 'multiplier'.

One may well·wonder, at this point, why it is that the national income fails to continue to increase beyond a certain level. Why does the multiplier effect 'work itself out' after a time? Why does national income settle down to stability at the new, higher level? The answer is that at each 'round' of spending, as investment workers pass their increased incomes to shopkeepers, shopkeepers to shop assistants, and so on, a certain proportion of the income received will be saved and only the remainder passed on, by spending, to the next stage in the multiplier process. If no such savings took place, there would be no upper limit to the level of income attained. The process would go on for ever; the size of the multiplier would be infinite.

It is only because people will not normally spend the whole of their incomes that the multiplier process has a definite limit. More than that, the size of the multiplier itself, and hence the total increase in income resulting from a given increase in investment expenditure, is determined by the proportion of their extra incomes which the people who benefit from the multiplier process decide to save. Let us denote the proportion of these extra 'marginal' incomes which is saved by the letter s, and assume, for simplicity, that everyone in the country saves this same proportion of his extra income. The size of the multiplier, usually denoted as 'k', is then given by a simple formula:

$$k = \frac{1}{s}.$$

It is easy to see that this formula is valid. If no one saves anything, s will equal o. Thus k will equal $\frac{1}{0} = \infty$. As we have already seen, the complete absence of savings will mean that there is no limit to the multiplier process; the multiplier is infinite. Similarly, if everyone saves the whole of his income, s will equal 1 and the multiplier will also equal 1. ($k = \frac{1}{1} = 1$). Income rises, as one would expect, by just the amount of investment expenditure.

In practice, the multiplier is never likely to reach either of these extremes. People will nearly always save something; and they will rarely save the whole of any increment in income. It is, of course, just possible that some people who receive an increment in income may increase their consumption by more than this amount. They might, for instance, expect that the rise in income was merely the forerunner of others. More usually, however, less than the whole of any increment of income will be spent. If everyone spends exactly $\frac{4}{5}$ of a marginal increment in income—in other words if they save just $\frac{1}{5}$ of that extra income—

$s = \frac{1}{5}$ and $k = \frac{1}{\frac{1}{5}} = 5$. The multiplier is 5, and a given increment of investment will give rise to a total increase in the national income which is five times as large. It follows that the *smaller* the proportion of the extra income that is saved (that is, the *larger* the proportion consumed), the larger the multiplier will be. If only $\frac{1}{1000}$ of any increase in income is saved, the multiplier will be 1000. If $\frac{99}{100}$ of any increase in income is saved, the multiplier will be in the region of one, to be exact $1\frac{1}{99}$.

This leads to some interesting conclusions. Where, as in a poor country, the percentage of any extra income that is saved is very low, the multiplier will be large. Small changes in investment activity in such poor countries, whether caused by Government investment or by changes in ordinary business investment, will result in violent alterations in the national income. Fortunately, with such a small degree of saving, even at the margin (when presumably many basic necessities of life have already been acquired), the bulk of such a poor community's industry must be producing consumption goods. The scope for autonomous changes in investment—and, indeed, the danger of unemployment itself—would be very small indeed. On the other hand, a very rich country might have high savings, and therefore a very low multiplier. But since only a small proportion of its total income would be spent on consumption goods, investment projects would be a very important form of economic activity. It would need a substantial increase in the size of an already large investment industry to bring about any marked increase in the national income. The late Lord Keynes reached the somewhat alarming conclusion that in modern industrialised countries the savings-consumption ratio is likely to be such that the multiplier will be big enough to cause sizable fluctuations in income if investment alters. At the same time the industries producing investment goods are likely to be large and all-embracing enough to make it difficult to find new investment projects easily when any deliberate increase in Government investment activity seems desirable.

The multiplier is a relatively passive phenomenon. It will not operate at all unless an initial change in the volume of investment takes place. In other words, the multiplier cannot operate unless there is something to be multiplied; and that something must be a change in investment. Moreover, whilst it is true that the multiplier amplifies the effect on income of any initial change in the level of investment, the fact that there are lags between the receipt and the spending of incomes tends to damp down economic fluctuations. For the total effects on national income of any change in investment are 'lagged'; they are spread over considerable periods of time. For instance, if investment first increases above a given level, and then quickly falls below it, the action of the multiplier will mean that income does not fluctuate so violently as investment has done. For the existence of time lags means that not all the multiplier effects of the increased investment will have worked themselves out by the time that investment falls below the original level. The remaining 'upward' multiplier effects will therefore cancel out some of the newer 'downward' ones and the oscillations in total income will be 'damped'. Again, the only way in which the size of the multiplier can change is by a spontaneous change in the proportion of their incomes that people save; and economists agree that such changes do not very often occur.

We know that changes in investment must be the main cause of any initial change in the level of a nation's income. In addition, however, investment will itself change *in response* to any change in the level of national income. Not only does the multiplier adjust consumption to the level of investment; the volume of investment itself fluctuates in response to changes in the level of the national income. Whenever the national income rises and extra goods are produced, there will be 'induced' investment in machinery and factories to produce these extra goods—whether they are consumption or capital goods. The mechanism by which such 'induced' investment is linked to changes in the level of the national income is known as the 'accelerator'.

In essence, the accelerator is simple. Let us assume that a light engineering industry, making consumer goods, has been operating at a given level of activity for a considerable time. Its only demands on the capital goods industry will therefore be to replace existing machinery as it wears out. This annual replacement demand will equal, say, 5 per cent of this light engineering industry's total stock of machines, assuming that each machine lasts for about twenty years. If the demand for the consumer goods produced by the light engineering industry now doubles, and if none of this extra demand can be met from surplus capacity in the industry, new investment goods must be bought. Should the whole of this capital equipment needed to meet the increased demand for the industry's product have to be produced within the following year, the machine-making industry's output would have to increase by twenty times during that particular year. It would have to meet the usual 5 per cent replacement demand and it would also have to double the light engineering industry's total capital equipment within one year. A relatively small change (of 100 per cent) in the demand for a given consumer good therefore causes an enormous increase (of 2000 per cent) in the output of the industry which supplies the machinery needed to make that consumer good. The 'acceleration principle' explains why there is this magnified increase in output and employment in the machine-making industry. The extent of such magnification shows whether the 'accelerator' is large or small. Similar magnified changes in the demand for capital goods have at times caused serious difficulties in, for example, the British textile machinery industry.

Now one clearly cannot expect the accelerator to work in any mathematically precise fashion—of the kind that our example would suggest. In the first place, we have assumed that the consumer good industry is unable to meet any of the increased demand for its produce without carrying out new investment—that there is no surplus capacity of any kind in the industry. At the same time, we have assumed that there is sufficient excess capacity in the capital goods industry to allow it to meet a twentyfold increase in the demand for the machines it makes.

Since our assumptions are unrealistic in this way, such a large accelerator as that suggested above is unlikely. Also, in practice, many economic fluctuations will be caused or accentuated by changes in business-men's expectations of the future, rather than by the 'accelerator', pure and simple. But it remains true that the acceleration principle helps to explain an important economic phenomenon. It shows that changes in 'induced' investment can be caused by changes in the level of the national income.

Our example shows why the accelerator depends on *changes* in income rather than on the absolute level of income. It is only *changes* in the demand for particular products that will produce these exaggerated repercussions on the industries which supply them with machinery and other capital goods. The illustration which we gave was, however, one showing how a change in the demand for *consumption* goods could affect the output of the industries producing capital goods. In practice, changes in the demand for investment goods will also have their accelerator effects. A change in the demand for a particular kind of capital good will have an effect on the output of the 'industries which produce capital goods for the capital goods industries', and so on. The accelerator thus depends on changes in the level of income, not merely consumption. It has to allow for the repercussions on investment of changes in the demand for both consumption *and* capital goods.

The 'accelerator' and the 'multiplier' between them have enabled Professor Hicks to produce an interesting explanation of economic fluctuations. Let us suppose that an economy which has been for some time at a low level of activity experiences an increase in investment. The multiplier, by itself, would mean that the level of income rose by a multiple of this increment of investment to a new and stable level. But the accelerator will operate too. Once the level of income begins to rise, because of the initial increase in investment, new investment will be 'induced' by the accelerator. This induced investment will lead to further multiplier effects, which in turn will create more induced investment. And superimposed upon these purely technical forces may be changed business expectations, as improved economic conditions breed optimism. These changed expectations may well themselves increase investment too. Provided that the initial increase in investment, the accelerator, the multiplier and the changed expectations of business-men between them represent a substantial motive force, the level of income and activity is likely to rise progressively until there is finally no possibility of further increase. The economy will hit the 'ceiling' of full employment, where production has reached the limits of capacity. We shall study the nature of this full employment 'ceiling', and the problems of inflation with which it is associated, in more detail at a later stage.

For the moment let us try to see why, unless some fresh stimulus is provided by a new spurt of industrial innovation and invention, or fresh action on the part of the Government, the economy is likely before long to relapse to a lower level of employment. The reason is a simple one. The economy has only hit the 'ceiling' because of the very rapid growth of induced investment during a sharp upward movement. Once the ceiling is reached, however, the rate at which the whole economy is progressing will inevitably diminish. The volume of induced investment will rise much less rapidly than it was doing during the up-swing and will finally start actually to decline. This 'turning point' will be reached for purely technical reasons. There are, however, two other factors which may assist in bringing about such a decline in investment—unless the Government is prepared to follow a deliberate policy of sustaining the level of investment activity in order to keep output at the maximum level.

The first is that in their desire to arrest the inflationary tendencies that are bound to appear in any economy which is producing to the limits of capacity, the monetary authorities may restrict credit. This will result in a rise in the rate of interest which will reduce investment. The multiplier and accelerator, working this time in a downward direction, will reduce the level of activity ; and it may not be possible to check investment activity at all without reducing it sharply. As we have seen, changes in business optimism are usually large, even exaggerated.

A second, similar, reason is that, even during a boom, business-men's expectations are likely, sooner or later, to take a turn for the worse.   In the light of history it is reasonable to argue that no boom can last for ever.   Thus, the longer prosperity continues, the more likely business-men are to feel that this prosperity will soon come to an end.   They may therefore give undue weight to relatively minor signs that a break in prosperity is in the offing. And we have already seen how 'mass opinion' on the Stock Exchange is prone to exaggerate any such signs of an impending change in the economy.

We have so far implied that 'investment' comprises the creation only of capital assets like machines and factories.   However, the building-up of stocks of raw materials and finished or semi-finished products represents an act of investment also.   This is particularly important in our present context.   There are two good reasons why the first result of any impending slump may be to reduce the rate of investment in stocks—and thus to lower the total level of investment in the economy as a whole.   First, stocks will act as a sensitive indicator of any change in consumer demand.   Firms will not normally adjust their output exactly and immediately to changes in demand; the whole purpose of stocks is to 'cushion' firms against random fluctuations in consumer demand.   But if, during a boom, such stocks should pile up above their 'normal' level, firms will not only regard this as a most unfavourable sign.   Their reaction will almost certainly be to reduce such stocks—to 'disinvest'.   This type of disinvestment is much more likely to occur in the initial phase of any depression than is a reduction in more long-term investment in plant and machinery; though as the slump proceeds this is likely to occur too.   Again, it is probable that business stocks will be more sensitive to changes in the rate of interest than will more long-term investment projects, which are more difficult to adjust rapidly to relatively small changes in interest rates.

The process that follows any such relatively minor down-turn is likely to proceed rapidly, and perhaps drastically.   The operation of the multiplier will reduce income by a multiple of the initial decline in investment.   This fall in income will in turn reduce induced investment;   and the whole process will be accompanied by pessimism, falling prices and profits, and consequently declining investment.   There will, however, be a definite lower limit to any such depression; there will be a 'floor' as well as a 'ceiling'.

Three major factors will determine the level of this 'floor'.

First, however bad a depression is, there is always likely to be a considerable volume of consumers' expenditure by private individuals. People, even if unemployed, must live, and they will eke out a rather unsatisfactory living perhaps by spending unemployment benefits, perhaps by drawing on their past savings. Second, there will be little reduction in Government expenditure during a depression ; indeed, in the modern economy the desire to prevent mass unemployment may well cause the amount of Government expenditure to rise. Third, there will be a certain amount of 'autonomous' expenditure on, for example, houses, roads and schools, whose volume will bear no very close relation to current economic conditions. These items between them will provide a solid bedrock of demand; and their existence will mean that, even in the worst slump, unemployment has a definite upper limit.

With induced investment, of course, it is another story. One fundamental peculiarity of induced investment may, indeed, prolong the depression. When an economy is moving in an upward direction, it will not be difficult for the economy to 'work the boom out of its system' because, at least in the long run, there is no clear upper limit to the possible volume of investment. In a downward direction there is. However bad a slump may be, the volume of investment cannot fall below zero—except in the sense that over time obsolescence and physical wastage will allow a certain measure of 'disinvestment' to take place, though relatively slowly. It follows that, by the very nature of investment, a boom may not last long because the investment goods industries will be able to supply even exaggerated demands for capital relatively quickly. But the economy may exhaust the employment-creating qualities of such investment quite rapidly, and find itself in a depression with an excessively large supply of capital. It may then take a great deal of time before the slow processes of physical deterioration and of obsolescence reduce this large capital stock to a level where it is insufficient to produce even the low level of output associated with the 'floor'. Thus, unless there is either some outside stimulus to autonomous investment, or the Government increases its expenditure, the economy may remain in depression for some time. Finally, however, automatic disinvestment is likely to proceed to the stage where a rise in replacement investment is essential; and this rise may well lead to accelerator and multiplier effects which bring a renewed burst of activity in the economy.

It should not, of course, be thought that all slumps will be major ones. It is possible, in particular, for a reduction in business stocks to cause a minor recession in activity. If stocks rise above what is considered a safe level, they will be reduced. But if Government spending and business investment in plant and machinery remain stable, and there is consequently no major fall in consumers' expenditure, the reduction of stocks will end when the 'normal' level of stocks is regained; the national income will increase once more. Such an 'inventory recession' was experienced throughout much of United States' industry in 1949, and also in Great Britain, particularly in the textile industry, in 1952.

We may now return to study the nature of the full employment 'ceiling'. The main problem is that complete full employment, in the sense of no one at all without a job, is impossible. There will always be some 'frictional' unemployment, because people are in the process of changing jobs. There may also be 'structural' unemployment, because particular industries have, in past booms, become larger than the economy can now sustain. It follows that the 'ceiling' will be reached before absolute, 100 per cent, full employment is attained. Additional complexities will arise if one considers other factors of production as well as labour. Shortages of raw materials or of power may mean that production stops expanding in some industries whilst there is still a considerable supply of labour available to them.

The simplest conception of the 'ceiling' is obviously that it is reached when the level of output in the economy is no longer able to respond to any increase in the type of demand that one meets with at this high level of employment. But unless labour is particularly mobile between industries, and unless *unused* capital equipment happens to be available in exactly the right proportions in the various trades, output may well fail to respond to changes in demand of the kind that we had been considering while many people in particular trades are still unemployed. At low levels of activity the main need may be to raise the aggregate demand for the products of the economy; when that level is high, it will much more often be necessary to increase the flexibility of the economy, so that labour shall not be completely unobtainable in some industries and yet abundant in others.

The main effect of the existence of this kind of 'ceiling' in any economy can be seen most easily from the way in which the general level of prices responds to changes in the aggregate level of demand. So long as the full employment ceiling has not been neared, there is likely to be little change in the general price level as the aggregate demand of the community increases. It is true that so long as individual firms are increasing their output towards the capacity level, unit costs will tend to fall somewhat. But since in conditions of growing prosperity wages and profits are likely to increase, it is probable that there will be little change in the general level of prices as the output of the whole economy rises.

Once the 'ceiling' is approached, however, prices will tend to rise as the total expenditure of the country continues to increase. Instead of expanding fairly readily in response to increasing aggregate demand, output will become 'sticky' in its response to rising expenditure; it will begin to do this even before output has reached the 'ceiling' and has therefore become completely unresponsive to demand changes. Some firms will find it necessary to increase output beyond the normal 'capacity' level and costs will rise. Other firms will experience shortages of labour, raw materials and so on. Ultimately these difficulties will mean that output ceases to increase at all in some industries although it is still increasing in others. The 'ceiling' will be low in some industries. Such rising costs and 'bottlenecks' in the supply of factors of production will mean that prices in general begin to rise, perhaps quite sharply, as the full employment 'ceiling' is approached. Rising costs will provide a good reason for price increases, and buoyant general demand will mean that business-men show little reluctance to making such increases.

Once full employment is achieved, and output is completely unresponsive to further changes in demand, the whole of any increase in national expenditure will be engaged in raising the price level. It is at this level of income that a clear-cut 'inflation' will begin; though the price rises that occur as full employment is neared can certainly be described as 'inflationary'. Economists have an old and respectable explanation of such inflation. This is the 'Quantity Theory of Money' which states that, when there is full employment, a given increase in the supply of money will cause an at least proportionate increase in the general price level.[1] At low levels of employment, as we have seen, an increase in the supply of money will lower the rate of interest and increase investment (and income); but it is unlikely to raise the price

[1] For a detailed discussion of the Quantity Theory of Money see *A Textbook of Economic Theory*, Stonier and Hague, pp. 473-478.

level. When full employment exists, any further rise in the supply of money, whilst it may lower the rate of interest, cannot increase output. It can only raise prices.

It follows that the general price level depends mainly on two factors—the level of output in the economy and the supply of money. We must now consider what determines the general level of money wages. It is clear that this will depend largely on the money supply. The supply of money will determine the rate of interest and hence the level of activity and employment. These, in turn, will affect the level of wages—not least because trade unions' bargaining power is likely to be greater when employment is high and labour is scarce. But the supply of money will also be connected with the wage level in a more direct way. Much money in the economy will mean high prices, and a high price level will usually imply a fairly high 'cost of living' and level of wages. The two main factors affecting the general level of money wages are the level of employment and the quantity of money.

The general level of *real* wages will depend mainly on the productivity of labour in terms of actual physical output. Where labour produces many goods and services in a given working week its *real* wage will be high, and vice versa. But the *real* wage of labour will depend on other factors too. Obviously, the higher the level of employment, the greater the volume of goods and services that can be bought by a country's workers. The real income of the working class *as a whole* is therefore bound to be greater the higher the level of output. But it does not follow at all that the real wage of an *individual* worker will change in this way. For when national output is low, employment is also low. Workers *who still have jobs* may well find that their real incomes are higher than when employment was high. For trade unions will probably succeed in ensuring that the rate of money wages does not fall far during a slump; and the prices of goods that workers buy may fall substantially—especially if imported goods are available much more cheaply because of a world-wide depression. Thus *employed* workers may find their real wages higher in depression than in times of prosperity. For the working class as a whole, the relation may be the opposite. To put the answer simply, the three really fundamental determinants of the real wages of the individual worker are: the level of employment, the general level of labour productivity in the country and the terms on which it can import foreign goods.

One may well wonder what effect trade unions have on the general level of wages. There can be no doubt that in the short run they will tend to keep money (and real) wages in both boom and slump above the level that would exist in their absence. In prosperity, their bargaining power will be strong, since businesses will be content to 'pass on' wage increases to consumers. In depression, though the workers' weakened bargaining position will prevent them obtaining *higher* wages, trade unions will prevent wages from 'sagging' as rapidly as they would in a competitive market.

On the other hand, evidence suggests that, before allowing for the effects of the deliberate redistribution of income, the *proportion* of the national income going to wage earners in, for example, Great Britain, has remained remarkably stable over the past fifty years. This has led people to wonder whether in the long run the effect of trade unions in altering the distribution of the national income may be negligible, and whether economic forces of a general and powerful nature do not overshadow the relatively puny actions of trade unions. It has also led economists, especially in France, to pose the leading question, whether perhaps trade unions would not be well advised to try to raise their living standard by engaging in political rather than economic battles. For example, they might press for income redistribution through family allowances or the 'Welfare State', rather than engage in the more traditional battle for higher wages in the labour markets for their own particular industries.

It should, however, be remembered that the size of labour's share in the national income cannot be considered in isolation. The real reward of labour depends to a very important degree on the productivity of the capital equipment which workers use. Highly productive plant and machinery means high real wages; but it may also mean, especially when the level of investment is high over a period of years, that a relatively high *proportion* of this high real national income represents a reward to those who own such capital assets.

So far, in dealing with the problems of inflation and depression, we have assumed that the Government takes no major part in influencing the level of activity in the community. We must now drop this assumption. Most modern communities accept, as a major aim of policy, the need to maintain a high and stable level of economic activity and employment. They attempt to ensure that the total spending of the community is large enough, but only just large enough, to buy all the goods which the fully employed community can produce at the current level of prices.

Let us see how a Government can deal with inflation and depression. There are, of course, several methods. The Government can increase or decrease the amount of money which it spends directly on consumption or investment goods; it can attempt to stimulate or reduce private investment by changes in the rate of interest. The main features of both these policies have, however, been discussed already. We shall concentrate our attention on a third possibility, namely, that the Government may deliberately unbalance its Budget and so raise or lower the level of national expenditure.

Let us consider a situation where there is inflation. Inflation occurs because the community is spending more money than is needed to purchase its full employment output at the existing price level. In other words, individuals and firms are not saving enough to prevent prices rising. Assuming that neither Government spending on goods and services nor private business outlay on investment goods is to be altered, the only solution is for 'Government savings' to be undertaken. If people and firms will not voluntarily save money for themselves, the Government must save it for them.

To determine the required volume of such 'Government savings', the extent of inflation must first be discovered. To do this, the Government must first make an estimate of the total value of the resources available for use within the country in the coming year, or whatever period of time is most suitable. Against this must be set the total value of the calls on these home resources which are expected during the following year—the total of expected expenditure on private consumption, private investment and on Government account.

The value of the resources available for use at home by any country will represent the total payments required by that community's factors of production if they are all to be induced to work; in other words, it represents the money value of all the goods and services that the fully employed community can produce—assuming that all prices remain constant and no further inflation occurs. To this total must be added any expected deficit on the balance of payments. For such a deficit means that foreign countries are lending resources to the community, which it can use to meet its home demand for goods and services.

For example, a balance of payments deficit of £500 million

would make extra resources worth that amount available to the country concerned. The total full employment value of the country's home resources, plus any expected balance of payments deficit, will therefore give the total value of resources available *for home use* in the period in question. It follows, conversely, that a given balance of payments *surplus* will *reduce* the resources available for home use by that amount. For in this case the community will be making some of its resources available to foreigners; and the resources available for use at home will be correspondingly diminished.

Having discovered the value of all the resources available to the country in a given period of time, the Government must make an estimate of the likely degree of inflation by calculating all the calls on these resources that are expected during the same time period. It must, in other words, add together expected private consumption expenditure, expected Government expenditure on consumer goods and expected investment activity by both the Government and by private individuals or firms. If, in the absence of any change in Government policy, these expected demands from consumers, business men and the Government together exceed the value of the resources available to meet them, inflation will occur—assuming, of course, that the estimates are accurate. The calculations may show that the total expected calls on resources (say £15,500 million) exceed the total value of those resources (say, £15,000 million) by £500 million. In this case an 'inflationary gap' exists. 'Inflationary pressure' to the tune of £500 million will be generated in the economy in the following year—unless the Government changes its fiscal or monetary policy.

What will be the result of this inflationary pressure? There are at least four possible ways in which it may affect the economy. First, an 'open' inflation may be allowed to take its own course and raise prices. Prices will then rise to such an extent that although consumers spend their projected £15,500 million, they will obtain only the same amount of goods and services as they could previously have bought for £15,000 million. The community's income will have remained completely unchanged in 'real' terms, though its *money* expenditure (and income) will have risen by £500 million.

Second, the inflationary pressure might exert its entire effects on the balance of payments. The community might acquire from abroad enough goods to satisfy its excessive demands. The high level of expenditure at home will mean a growing demand for imports; export goods will also be diverted towards the home market. Post-war experience has shown that this is an extremely likely result of domestic inflation. But it represents only a temporary palliative. A balance of payments deficit can only be financed by selling gold and foreign exchange reserves, or by selling overseas investments; and such reserves are never unlimited.

A third, again likely, result of the existence of inflationary pressure is that rationing and/or price control may be introduced in an attempt to prevent prices from rising and to 'suppress' the inflation. In this way the Government can keep down consumption expenditure to the total sum expected. The result will be shortages, queues and all the usual signs of scarcity. Unfortunately, such a 'suppressed inflation' rarely remains 'suppressed' for long or in all directions. There is little likelihood that consumers will put more of their money into savings. Quite apart from any other factors, the very existence of inflation will make it seem foolish to save money at a time when rising prices mean that it becomes worth less, in real terms, every day. Again, if the incomes of some sections of society lag significantly behind the rising prices, they will be too busy trying to cling to their old-established standards of living to be able to save more.

Because of such facts, people will look for ways to spend their money *now*. To 'suppress' the inflation will merely be to divert spending away from the basic sectors of the economy, where price controls are likely to be energetically enforced, to firms producing 'luxuries', where price control is less enthusiastic. It is not easy to control all the prices in the modern economy, and, at any rate in the less 'essential' industries, price control schemes are likely to break down to a greater or smaller degree in the face of a persistent inflationary 'gap'. Many prices will rise. Labour and capital will be diverted from basic industries, where prices (and wages) are kept down, towards those producing 'non-essential' goods, where high wages can be earned. This kind of situation may conceivably be typical only of immediate post-war periods; it certainly occurred in Britain after 1945. But it may also happen more generally. No one yet knows.

Fourth, just as private investment or Government expenditure on consumption or investment goods may be deliberately increased to combat a depression, so they may be deliberately reduced in an inflation, particularly since the Government can usually exert a fairly simple and exact control over the total size of both its own expenditure and business investment. A cut in Government expenditure will mean that some wants which were previously satisfied communally are now satisfied privately—or not at all. This may not necessarily be undesirable. A cut in business investment, however, will usually be unambiguously undesirable. Increased investment in the present will be an important source of increased productivity, and hence a higher standard of living in the future. Admittedly, the community must somehow maintain the difficult balance between present consumption on the one hand, and investment intended to increase productive efficiency and to provide more consumer goods in the future, on the other. But one suspects that in conditions of long-period inflation there is more danger that too little investment of this type will be carried out rather than too much.

It should, of course, be remembered that these various effects of inflation will rarely occur separately. A combination of them all is quite likely. Prices are almost certain to rise somewhat, though probably not fast enough to absorb all the excess purchasing power, so that some shortages will develop. A worsening of the balance of payments position is almost certain, and it is likely that the volume of investment will fall below expectations —if only because delivery dates have to be pushed back.

In other words, if left to its own devices, the inflationary pressure will work its way out of the system—but only at the expense of rising prices, queues, cuts in rations and investment, and a weakening foreign exchange position. It would be far better if the inflationary pressure could be removed before it had any chance to cause such tribulations.

This is precisely what monetary and fiscal policy can do. As we have seen, a rise in the rate of interest will reduce investment. But the 'multiplier' and 'accelerator' effects of this may cause a serious decline in activity, and modern economists are neither entirely agreed nor particularly optimistic about the potentialities of monetary policy.

An alternative (or perhaps complementary) policy is that of 'disinflationary budgeting'. Here the Government aims just to remove, by budgetary policy, an amount of income just equal to the 'inflationary gap'. Inflation is thereby prevented, but no deflationary pressure is created in its place. The essence of such a budgetary policy is that the Government should aim at

H

providing a budget surplus just large enough to make up the difference between what the community is expected to spend and the resources available for it to spend its money on.

The precise nature of this budget surplus is, however, of importance. When making its calculations of total expected national investment expenditure the Government will normally include in them capital expenditure undertaken by the Government. It follows that capital items should be left out of account in calculating the Government's budget surplus. Otherwise there will be double-counting. It is the excess of *current* income over *current* expenditure which must be made equal to the inflationary gap. It follows, too, that when framing his budget, and attempting to provide for a surplus of this particular size, the Chancellor of the Exchequer cannot make use of taxes that will be paid out of peoples' savings. The community's savings are already insufficient; it is consumption spending which must be mopped up by the increased taxes that are levied in order to create a budget surplus.

All that has been said above applies in reverse to an attempt to prevent a depression. We have seen earlier that a reduction of the rate of interest and an increase in Government investment expenditure will, if large enough, cause multiplier effects that will enable full employment to be achieved. We may now note that the multiplier effects of any such Government investment depend on the way in which that investment is financed. In the earlier discussion in this chapter we assumed that the investment in question was financed by a budget deficit. If, however, the expenditure is financed, wholly or partly, by taxation on consumption, the size of the multiplier will be correspondingly reduced. For if the 'multiplier' consumption expenditure which flows from the increase in investment activity merely replaces existing consumption expenditure, the only net addition to the national income will be the additional investment outlay itself. In such a situation the size of the multipler will always be one.

Since any sizeable multiplier effects from Government investment expenditure depend on that expenditure being financed from a budget deficit, it is only a short step to using a budget deficit as a deliberate instrument of Government policy to cure a depression. The position is exactly the reverse of the one outlined above for curbing inflation. The Government must first calculate the extent to which total expected national expenditure in the following year is expected to fall short of the level required to give full employment. This will show the size of the expected 'deflationary gap'—the extent of expected 'deflationary pressure' in the economy. Having made this discovery, it remains only for the Government to aim at a budget *deficit* of that size, by reducing taxes again on consumption and not on savings.

Sometimes Governments will wish to use monetary and budgetary policy simultaneously to cure depression or inflation. This means that any surplus on the budget need not bear the whole burden of the attack on inflation. The Government can reduce the size of the budget surplus (or deficit) which it aims at by an amount which will depend on the results which it expects to gain from its monetary policy during the ensuing year.

CHAPTER X

PUBLIC FINANCE

WE have just considered one particular aspect of Government economic policy—the rôle of a budget surplus or deficit in preventing fluctuations in the level of economic activity. We now consider the more general problems of public finance, namely, what are the main factors which determine the size and nature of Government expenditure, and how is that expenditure financed ?

In some respects, at least, the Chancellor of the Exchequer is a very lucky man. He is one of the few people who are able to decide just how much money they will spend in the coming year (barring accidents), and then, later, decide how to finance that expenditure. This, of course, is a slight exaggeration of the truth. At most times the size of Government expenditure will be fixed with at any rate half an eye on the revenue commitments that it implies. Nevertheless, it is usual to begin the task of framing the nation's budget by first of all setting out the proposed Government expenditure.

Economic principles play only a minor part in determining the size of Government expenditure. It has long been accepted that there are three major fields for legitimate Government outlay, and in each it would be difficult to find any very clear economic principles by which one could decide the amount of money to be spent. First, it is now generally agreed that the Government alone is able to provide armed forces that are adequate to meet any attack by a foreign power. To provide for the common defence has long been accepted as a major rôle of any Government; and such defence continues, unfortunately, to be necessary today. Since 1939 a major part of Government expenditure in most countries has been devoted to maintaining military strength.

Second, the Government must spend money to ensure an efficient and just internal administration. In every country law and order must be preserved internally, through the police force, and the creation and maintenance of an equitable legal system. Equally important is the provision of an efficient administrative system at the level of both central and local government. Spending on this second rôle of the modern Government will rarely represent a very substantial proportion of total Government expenditure ; but it provides the foundation of a stable society.

The third broad field for Government spending is concerned with social and economic ends. Education, pensions, family allowances, health services, all such social services represent a field in which governments are generally acknowledged to be able to perform a function which no private individual or organisation can fulfil. There are also many economic projects, for example, the building of roads and other communal construction works, where the Government is able to carry out investment projects which are of great benefit to the community, but which would not offer sufficiently profitable prospects to make them attractive to ordinary business men.

It should be apparent, from the nature of Government spending, that there is no simple economic criterion by which the amount and the distribution of such spending can be decided. Economists agree that *in theory* Government expenditure should be so allocated that the last pound spent on each type of project gives the same 'social benefit'. For if the 'benefit', the satisfactions, derived by society from the last pound spent on, say, jet fighters is considerably lower than that derived from the last pound spent on free school meals, the total welfare of the community would be increased by a reallocation of expenditure, with less spent on aircraft and more on school meals.

In practice, of course, any such close calculation of the 'social benefit' derived from spending an extra, 'marginal', pound in any direction is quite impossible. So, whilst the aim of the Government should perhaps, in theory, be to equate the 'social benefit' derived from the last pound spent in each direction, such a policy cannot be pursued in practice.

Nor, of course, can it be assumed that all governments will wish to follow the economist's predilection and try to achieve the maximum possible satisfactions for the community as a whole. Most governments will be prone to favour sectional interests. A government may expand agricultural subsidies for purely political reasons. Trade unions may press for increased state pensions at the expense of naval re-equipment. Decisions on the scale and direction of Government expenditure will always be so bedevilled by political considerations that any logical economic explanation will often be out of the question.

Assuming that the size and nature of Government expenditure is decided on, however, it will be possible to work out the necessary amount of Government revenue—allowing for any budget deficit or surplus that 'disinflationary budgeting' may require. How can such revenue be obtained? In the absence of inflation, there are two main sources : taxation, and borrowing by making new issues of long-term bonds on the Stock Exchange. Taxation, in turn, comprises income taxes, commodity taxes and capital taxes.

Borrowing can be discussed briefly and it will be best to do this now. There has been a traditional objection to any form of large-scale revenue-raising by the British Government. In the sixteenth century the cry was 'The King must live of his own'. Only very recently has the saying 'The best budget is the smallest budget' died a timely death. There always have been, and still are, many people who are prepared to argue that *by definition* any form of Government activity will be carried out less efficiently than that of private individuals. But the objections to Government borrowing have been even stronger. Especially in countries with a strong Protestant tradition, state borrowing has been regarded as a highly iniquitous type of activity. Only during time of war, when it was clearly impossible to finance all Government expenditure from taxation, was large-scale borrowing though reputable.

At present the climate of opinion seems to be changing. The vast scale of borrowing during two world wars has broken down most moral and political objections to Government borrowing. The general agreement, itself in part a result of war-time experience, that Governments *can* maintain full employment if they follow the type of budgetary policy outlined in the previous chapter, has led to the realisation that full employment may often be obtainable only at the price of budget deficits, and consequent Government borrowing. It is now widely agreed, therefore, that if the policy of 'disinflationary budgeting' at a given time requires a budget deficit of a given size, then this particular amount of Government borrowing is an inevitable consequence of the desire for full employment, and must be accepted as such.

Most economists are prepared to agree that, over relatively short periods of time, the results of such a policy cannot be serious. Indeed, since the borrowing maintains the level of employment, it will be socially desirable. But economists are much less certain about the long-term results of Government borrowing. If during, say, the remainder of the twentieth century the British or American Government had to run a considerable budget deficit year after year, this could mean that a serious problem arose in paying interest on the vast total of debt that might well be accumulated over some forty years. It is true that, in a sense, since the transaction would be an internal one for the country in question, there would be no real 'burden'. Money would, so to speak, be taken from one pocket in the community and put into another, in a way that would not happen if the debt interest had to be paid in gold, or foreign currency, to another country. Yet might not the level of taxation needed to finance debt interest payments accumulated over many years become so high as to be disastrous? Most economists agree that this is a potential problem, but point to two ways out.

First, it is by no means certain that the pursuit of full employment means a permanent and large budget deficit. Second, provided the national income continues to grow at a moderate but steady rate, with rising productivity, there is no reason why even a substantial annual budget deficit should cause debt interest payments to represent a growing *proportion* of the national income. The real danger would arise where the national income was constant; and it is just such constancy of the national income which any sane full employment policy will aim to avoid. The whole object will be, by keeping the economy at all times pushing up against the full employment 'ceiling', to ensure a progressive rise of the national income. For a rise in productivity, and hence in the level of the 'ceiling', will be the only possible method of raising standards of living.

Whatever the country, the main source of Government revenue in normal times will be taxation, and the main taxes those on income and those on commodities. In Great Britain each of these taxes at present raises roughly the same total amount of revenue, and this has been so for many years.

The main feature of income taxes is that they will usually be 'progressive'—they will take a higher proportion of large incomes than of small ones. This means that the 'marginal' rate of tax, the rate of tax on an extra pound of income, will increase as the taxpayer's income rises. This type of tax accords with modern ideas of social justice. The richer one is, the argument runs, the greater is one's responsibility to help to satisfy the community's 'collective wants' by helping to finance Govern-

ment expenditure.   More than this there is, in Britain, a conventional minimum level of income, based on the size of the
taxpayer's family and his personal responsibilities, below which
no income tax is levied at all.   Above this minimum level, the
British income tax system is at present highly 'progressive'.

The progressiveness of the modern income-tax system has
two main economic effects.   First, it 'redistributes' the national
income from rich to poor.   Money which is paid in taxation by
the relatively rich is paid to poorer people in the form either of
direct cash payments—family allowances, health and unemployment benefits, etc.,—or of payments in kind—free medical
attention, free education, subsidised food, and so on.

That progressive taxation automatically redistributes the
national income should be obvious.   In any modern society, the
number of people paying large sums of money in income tax
will be small.   It follows that even if these well-to-do taxpayers
received back in cash or kind as much as everyone else in the
country, they would be paying for far more than their own share
of the benefits derived from Government spending.   For the
poor would be paying so much less.   In fact, of course, the
relatively rich will probably receive less, in cash and kind, from
the Government, than the poor.   The rich taxpayer may well
have fewer children and thus receive smaller family allowances;
he may send his children to school as fee-paying scholars instead
of allowing them to go to 'free' schools, and so on.   A progressive
tax system redistributes income, directly or indirectly, from rich
to poor.

Two results of redistributive taxation are worth noting.   First,
the degree of equality in post-tax incomes will be much greater
than that of pre-tax incomes.   Whether such equality is desirable in any moral or economic sense is a very different question,
the answer to which we shall consider later.   Second, the result
of such greater equality of post-tax incomes will probably be to
raise the proportion of the national income that is consumed.
Where the redistribution of the national income takes place by
the provision of a service *in kind* for the poor, there is no possibility that the recipient will save anything.   The Government
has already spent the money for him.   But even where the Government merely takes money from the rich and gives it in the form
of *cash* to the poor, the proportion of this income that is spent
on consumer goods is likely to be higher than if the rich man had
spent the money for himself.   The poor, being so near the mini-

mum subsistence level, will have little margin for savings; the
rich will almost certainly save something.

This provides an economic argument for the redistribution
of income in times of depression. If money is redistributed from
rich to poor, the proportion of income consumed will rise. This
will mean a rise in consumption expenditure and hence in the
national income. It is possible, for example, that the extent of
income redistribution in Britain after 1945 has been one reason,
though only one, why full employment was maintained with so
much less difficulty than in the early 1920's.

The second main economic feature of progressive income
taxation is its effects on incentives to work and to invest. We
consider, first, the way in which it will affect the amount of work
done by an individual worker. This can be analysed, in the
same way as the effect of increased wages was in Chapter V, by
studying income and substitution effects.

If there have previously been no taxes, and a progressive
income tax is now introduced, the first result will be to lower
the relative price of leisure. It will become 'cheaper'. Instead
of having to sacrifice an extra 3s. income if he works one hour
less, the worker may now only sacrifice, say, 2s. The other
shilling would have gone to the Government in tax. The 'pure'
substitution effect of this change will lead the worker to take
more of the 'cheaper' good—leisure—and less of the other, more
normal, consumption goods that he buys. So far, the income
tax will unambiguously reduce incentives to work.

As we saw in Chapter V, however, the income effect will not
work in the same way. If a reduction could be made in the taxpayer's income, in a way which did *not* alter the 'price' of leisure
vis-à-vis other goods, for example, by levying a lump sum ('poll')
tax, the taxpayer would almost certainly reduce the amount of
leisure he took. Since his 'real' income has fallen, the taxpayer
will tend to buy less of all the 'goods' available to him—including
leisure.

The effect on incentives to work when a progressive income
tax is imposed can now be seen. It is unlikely that this income
tax will induce workers receiving relatively low wages to alter
the amount of work they do. The rates of tax they pay will be
too low. Only during and after the 1939–45 war does it seem
probable that *unskilled* workers in Britain were paying sufficiently
high tax rates for there to be any significant 'disincentive effect'
as a result of income taxation. The low tax rates mean that

there is no widespread tendency for workers to substitute leisure for income; taxation changes the 'price' of leisure so little. At the same time any income effect there may be works in the opposite direction—a lower real income impelling a reduction in the amount of leisure.

It is with the higher-paid, or skilled, workers that significant changes in the amount of work done are likely to result from levying progressive income taxes. The rates of tax are likely to be high enough to cause a significant reduction in the 'price' of leisure. In post-war Britain, for example, the rate of tax on the 'marginal' income of such skilled workers has often been between 30 and 40 per cent of an extra 'marginal' hour's earnings. The whole problem, of course, arises from the progressiveness of the tax system. It is the extra hour's work in any day or week which bears the *highest* rate of tax.

With such high rates of tax, the substitution effect is likely to be strong. A fall of 40 per cent in the 'price' of leisure can obviously be significant. The worker might, therefore, if income taxation only had a substitution effect, reduce the number of hours he worked quite substantially. The income effect, how-ever, will again work in the opposite direction and will tend to reduce the amount of leisure that the worker takes. But one cannot rely on the income effect to cancel out the substitution effect. It is much less predictable. A good reason for suppos-ing that income effects will *not* cancel out substitution effects is that, if income effects did usually cancel out substitution effects, economists would not have regarded this problem of the disincen-tive effects of income taxation as a serious one for post-war Britain.

With a progressive income tax, then, the higher-paid worker may well work fewer hours than he would in the absence of any taxes. The most serious effects on incentives to work, however, are likely to occur with highly paid business executives and pro-fessional men. A progressive tax system can mean that 50 to 75 per cent of the 'marginal' earnings of such men (at any rate in Britain) may have to be paid in taxes. The substitution effects of such high tax rates will obviously be exceptionally strong, and, again, one cannot rely on the income effect to cancel them out. Fortunately, these types of worker are likely to be interested in their work for its own sake; but even so the very high marginal rates of tax are likely to take their toll. The disincentive effects of high income taxes are, perhaps, even more acute for the owner of the one-man business. He has to pay heavy rates of income tax—and he may well have to pay profits tax too. On the other hand, he can probably persuade the tax authorities to allow more of his income as a tax-free payment for 'expenses'.

A progressive income tax, then, must often result in some reduction of incentives to work. But one obviously cannot be certain how important these effects will be in the economy as a whole.

It is often claimed that high income taxes will also reduce the willingness of private individuals to lend money to firms that are entering on new investment projects. For any dividends that the lenders receive will be taxed. It is doubtful whether one should put much weight on such an argument. The alternatives to lending are, on the one hand, to hoard one's savings in the form of cash, and, on the other hand, not to save at all. We have already seen why there is great doubt whether changes in interest rates play much part in determining the level of savings. Similarly, it is by no means certain that a reduction through taxation in the post-tax rate of return on securities would cause many people to hold their savings in the form of cash instead of buying securities.

Let us consider a situation where taxation is high in order to pay for rearmament, and where the high tax rates are a concomitant of mild inflation caused by the Government expenditure on arms. In such circumstances there will be little to encourage people to hold actual cash; it will be losing value slowly as time passes. The alternatives of holding either bonds or equities will have their attractions, despite the fact that their yields will be subject to tax. It is true that when the man who has bought bonds comes to turn them into cash, the money which their sale gives him will itself have lost some of its value through inflation. But bonds do at least offer a return, however small, in the shape of interest payments. And with Government expenditure, and hence the supply of money, at a high level, a *rise* in the rate of interest is unlikely. Bond prices are unlikely to fall, and there is therefore little danger of capital losses for investors.

There may, however, be definite and positive advantages in holding equities during times of inflation. For the general buoyancy of the economy will mean that their dividend yield is likely to be high. More than this, the fact that there is inflation as well as high taxes will mean that the money value of firms' physical assets is likely to be rising steadily. This will lead to a corresponding rise in the price of equities. For the value of the latter will always bear a close relationship to the value of the physical assets of the firms who have issued them. The investor in equities consequently has strong reasons, in times of inflation, for hoping that he will reap capital gains; and these will not be subject to income tax. It is true that a profits tax may be super-imposed on the income tax so that the dividend yield of an equity bears an even higher rate of tax than does the interest earned from bond holdings. Nevertheless, the prospect of possible (untaxed) capital gains from holding equities may well mean that high taxes on the dividend yields of equities do not cause the supply of 'risk capital' to dry up significantly during times of inflation. Such a 'drying up' is what many British economists and business-men have feared during the inflationary post-war years.

This does not, of course, mean that high tax rates will have *no* effect on the way in which people distribute their savings between cash hoards, bonds and equities. It merely suggests that any such effect will probably be slight when there are also inflationary conditions in the economy.

When there is no inflation, it is unlikely that tax rates will be so high. But even if they are, it is not certain that this will have any serious results on the supply of capital to industry. For the fact that there is no inflation shows that there is no shortage of savings. Indeed there may well be too much saving, and consequently unemployment. High income and profits taxes can therefore have no very serious general effects on the economy, even if they *do* reduce saving.

We must now consider the nature and the effects of taxes on commodities. These will normally take one of two forms. Either a sales tax will be levied on a good or service at the moment when it is sold, as, for example, when a tax is levied on each motor-car or each packet of cigarettes sold; or else a licence fee will be levied at given intervals during the life of the article, as with wireless and television licences. We shall concentrate on the former type of tax—the sales tax.

The term 'sales tax' probably needs further explanation. Economists use this term in a very general sense. To them it means any tax that is levied on a good at the moment when that good is bought. The British purchase tax, which takes the form of a percentage addition to the wholesale price of the good in question, is one particular type of sales tax. Similarly, the British customs and excise duties, levied on goods like tobacco, are 'sales taxes' from the economist's point of view. Although many customs and excise duties take the form of import duties, they are intended to have exactly the same general effects as any other sales tax; they aim at raising revenue by altering the price of the taxed good.

Let us now consider the effects of the introduction of a sales tax on a given article. The most obvious result is that the price of the good is bound to rise; but it need not rise by the whole of the amount of the tax. For the second result of the tax will be to reduce the output of the good. People will not be willing to buy as much as when the price was lower, and the output of the good will therefore fall. This fall in output will mean that some firms previously producing the good now cease to do so. These firms may well, in a competitive industry, be the least efficient firms, so the price (after the tax has been paid) that is needed to give 'normal' profits to the industry will be lower than before the tax was levied. The firms remaining in the industry, being more efficient than the 'marginal' firms that have been driven out, will be content with a lower 'post-tax' price. Consequently, the price to the consumer will not rise by the whole of the amount of the tax.

The extent to which the price of a taxed good will rise in any given circumstances will depend on the nature of the prevailing demand and supply conditions. The more inelastic the demand by consumers, the more willing they are to allow prices to rise and yet not restrict their purchases, the greater is the rise in the price paid by consumers likely to be. On the other hand, the more inelastic the supply of the product is, the less able firms in the industry are to move into other industries, the greater will be the fall in post-tax receipts that producers are willing to suffer.

Thus, in competitive industries, prices will rise little where taxes are levied on goods that have many substitutes, and hence an elastic demand by consumers. The price rise will also be small where the firms producing these taxed goods cannot produce any other goods at all, so that the supply is highly inelastic. For, in these conditions, producers will have to see a very serious fall in the post-tax price they receive before they will be induced to leave the industry. Similarly, where the demand of consumers is very unresponsive, inelastic, to price changes, and where suppliers can easily find other uses for their factories if the price they receive falls, the price of the commodity will rise by an amount almost equal to the size of any tax that is levied.

The same factors will determine whether or not the imposition of a tax will cause a substantial change in the output of the taxed commodity. Where demand and supply are both elastic, so that consumers can find many substitutes for the taxed good, and where producers can easily produce alternative goods, the imposition of a tax will cause a large shrinkage in an industry's output. Where consumers cannot easily find alternative goods to purchase, and where producers have no easy alternative uses for their factories, output will contract little because both demand and supply will be inelastic. Such effects on output must always be in the mind of Governments when they levy taxes. In normal times Governments will be unwilling to cause any serious reduction in the output of any industry, since this may mean unemployment for some of its workers. On the other hand, if the Government wishes to acquire resources for its own use, say for building tanks or electronic equipment, it may well be anxious to tax, say, the motor-car or the radio industries in order to free productive resources which can then be used to turn out these things.

When there is monopoly or oligopoly the results of levying sales taxes will be similar. Output is almost certain to fall; prices are likely to rise. In oligopoly there is likely to be a tacit agreement between producers to raise prices in order to recoup the tax payments, though, as with the wage rise on page 57, the tax increase might be absorbed. In monopoly, too, the sole producer will often find it profitable to increase his prices to make up for the tax. This rise in prices may indeed be very substantial if a monopolist is benefiting from increasing returns as he expands the scale of his output. If the tax reduces the monopolist's output, it may raise production costs per unit of output and thus require a substantial rise in his prices to cover these higher costs. Indeed, the more rapidly a monopolist's costs are falling as his output rises, the greater would be the rise in price that the imposition of a tax on his product would cause.

We have so far studied the effects of a sales tax on the price and output of the taxed commodity. These effects between them will, of course, determine the amount of revenue raised from taxing the commodity, and it is this revenue which will be of particular interest to the Chancellor of the Exchequer. It is true that the effects of taxes on prices and output will often be important to the Government; but the main object of a tax is to raise money. It follows from what has been said so far that a given amount of money can be raised most simply by imposing taxes on goods with either inelastic demands or inelastic supplies —or both.

It seems likely that, in practice, the *supplies* of most goods will be moderately responsive to changes in their prices. With manufactured goods, say cigarettes, a factory whose sales are seriously reduced by a tax on tobacco is likely to find it quite simple to produce an alternative good—if necessary by scrapping its existing machines and buying new ones. Similarly, a tax on an agricultural product like sugar beet would leave farmers free to grow many alternative crops. Thus it is probable that the Chancellor of the Exchequer is likely to find little reason, on the supply side, for taxing one good rather than another.

With demand, however, things are different. The demand for some goods is markedly less elastic than for others. Some have close substitutes ; others do not. It will therefore be possible to raise a given amount of money most easily by taxing those goods which have the most inelastic demands. A tax will have little effect on total sales, and a given rate of tax will raise more money than with other goods, whose more elastic demands mean that sales would have fallen off more substantially when the tax was imposed.

The types of good on which sales taxes have been levied in Britain during the past century have been determined by such considerations. In the second half of the nineteenth century, taxes on goods like tea and sugar were important sources of revenue. The demand for these commodities was inelastic ; and since *all* rates of tax were low, there were no strong objections to a tax which probably tended to bear rather more heavily on the poor than on the rich. Since 1918, and especially since 1939, the position has changed radically. The large amount of revenue needed has raised all tax rates to fairly high levels. Public opinion is also against taxes on 'necessities' like sugar, tea or bread ; and all these are goods with inelastic demands. The Chancellor of the Exchequer has therefore been forced to turn to the taxa- tion of 'conventional necessities' like beer and tobacco. People regard these goods as so important to life that they continue to buy them in much the same amounts as before, even after high taxes have been levied on them. At the same time, there are no social objections to taxes on these goods as there are with foodstuffs.

This leads us to the question, 'Are incomes taxes "better"

in any sense, than sales taxes?' Economists have in the past tended to hold the view that income taxes are preferable. In the world as we know it, it is unusual for *sales* taxes to be levied at the same rate on *all* goods. An income tax, however, means a reduction in income with the prices of all goods left constant. Thus an income tax reduces 'real' income after tax; but it leaves the relative prices of *all* ordinary consumer goods un-altered. Sales taxes alter these relative prices and therefore cause 'substitution effects' as well. Consumers not only suffer a reduction in real income; they also have to reorganise their purchases to take account of the new price structure.

This latter distortion gives rise to an 'excess burden' of indirect taxation. There will be, the conventional argument runs, a greater loss of satisfaction for consumers if a given sum of money is levied by a sales tax on any good, or group of goods, than if exactly the same amount is levied by an income tax. The extra loss of satisfaction represents the 'excess burden' of indirect taxation.

This view was appropriate enough in the early years of the twentieth century, at which time it was widely accepted. For tax rates were low, and whilst sales taxes distorted consumers' choices between the available consumer goods, income taxes did not lower the 'price' of leisure sufficiently to cause serious dis-incentive effects. With the higher tax rates of the post-1939 era, however, British economists are agreed that income taxes can also have these distorting effects. By reducing the price of leisure, they cause an excess burden as compared with a tax, for example a 'poll' (lump sum) tax, which levies the same amount of money and thereby reduces the taxpayer's real income, but leaves the 'price' of leisure unaltered and therefore causes no 'substitution effect'.

There is thus less agreement nowadays about the respective merits of sales taxes and income taxes. In the days when all taxes were low, it was clearly unlikely that there would be any serious disincentive effects from income taxes. But even with low tax rates, the sales taxes levied on some commodities were likely to be at higher rates than on others. As we have seen, goods with highly inelastic demands appear particularly desir-able objects of taxation. Their sales will remain roughly constant whatever the rate of any taxes levied on them, so that the total tax yield from a relatively moderate rate of tax will be both high and predictable. At the same time, however, since the amount of the good bought is not very sensitive to taxation, there will be less distortion of the pattern of consumers' expenditure—and therefore there will be a smaller 'excess burden' than if goods with elastic demands are taxed.   Nevertheless, there will still be *some* 'excess burden' from levying such sales taxes, and income taxes will be superior to them.

Where tax rates are high, however, the position is different. As we have seen, income taxes can then cause serious disincentive effects; and these effects could be avoided by the (politically unacceptable) poll tax.   In these circumstances, it may be possible to raise revenue more effectively by sales taxes instead of income taxes.   Sales taxes themselves will also cause people to work less hard than they would have done in the absence of taxation.   For the 'price' of leisure will be lowered if the income earned from doing an extra hour's work can only be spent on goods which are now dearer, because sales taxes have been levied on them.   Thus when sales taxes are introduced there will usually be 'disincentive effects'.

Nevertheless, if the highest sales taxes are levied, in the form of entertainments taxes, on, say, cricket matches and theatre tickets, people may do more work than if the same amount of revenue were raised by an income tax.   For workers will need less leisure if the high prices of such entertainments induce them to patronise the entertainments less often.   Some of the bad effects of sales taxes in distorting the price structure in the economy may therefore be offset.   The Government may be able, through the selection of goods that must be enjoyed at leisure to bear the highest rates of sales tax, to make people work more.   For work becomes relatively 'cheaper' compared with leisure if those goods which are enjoyed at leisure are more heavily taxed than the others.   And when work becomes 'cheaper' more of it will be done.

When general rates of tax are high, sales taxes have two other advantages.   First, there is the important administrative convenience that sales taxes are not easy to evade.   Income taxes can be avoided by failing to declare income, and by obtaining large tax-free 'expense' allowances.   At high rates of tax, great rewards will be gained from such tax evasion, 'legal' or illegal, and there will therefore be more of it.   Sales taxes, however, cannot be avoided unless the person who collects the tax from the consumer, perhaps a shopkeeper, breaks the law— a rather less likely occurrence.

I

There is also the political advantage that by levying extra sales taxes the Government may be able, surreptitiously, to reduce the degree of progressiveness in the country's tax system and thus reduce the disincentive effects of highly progressive tax rates. High sales taxes may be levied on 'conventional necessities' like cigarettes, which have inelastic demands, and which are also bought in significant amounts by relatively poor people. The rate of tax on people with low incomes would thereby be raised; and yet no one would be able to prove exactly what the nature of the changes in the tax system had been. For no one could show this, for a whole community, without knowing every individual's purchases of taxed goods—an impossible feat. Yet if higher *income* taxes were levied on the poor, everyone would be aware of this immediately, merely from studying the income-tax laws.

It follows that there is no *general* case either for income tax or for sales taxes. Each has its advantages, and in any given situation a judicious mixture of the two will usually produce the desired effects. It is worth noting, for example, that whilst in backward countries it might seem desirable to finance Government spending by levying no taxes except income taxes and imposing these on the rich and the rich alone, this would not be possible in an undeveloped country whose tax-collection system was inefficient. In such a country the use of sales taxes may well provide the only way of raising any money at all; particularly if standards of honesty and literacy are low. More than this, the lack of efficient and honest tax collectors *within* a backward country may also mean that the only effective method of levying even a sales tax is to do so at the ports, by taxes on both imports *and* exports, often on goods like tea.

Finally, a word about capital taxes. It is not usual for these to yield an important proportion of a country's revenue, and for good reasons. As we have seen, there is no point, in inflation, in trying to provide the Government with revenue by taxing people's past savings. The need is to *increase present savings*. It was therefore pointless to argue, as some people in Britain did immediately after 1945, that a 'capital levy' was the cure for inflation. The real cause of that inflation was excessive spending—and an attack on either past or present savings could do nothing to reduce current spending. Indeed, if such a capital levy had been regarded as the forerunner of more similar levies in the future, it might well have encouraged people to live beyond their current incomes, spend their capital and thereby ensure that they, and not the Exchequer, reaped the benefits from their past thriftiness. Unless the public can be convinced that any capital levy is only a once-for-all expedient, its results may well be to worsen, and not to improve, an already inflationary situation.

Capital taxes would, in a sense, have more point in times of slump. If, in depression, the Government finances its expenditure wholly out of past (or present) savings, the multiplier effects of that Government spending will be as great as possible. In a slump, however, it is usually politically and administratively simpler to finance the Government's spending out of a straightforward budget deficit. Thus, in inflation, when more taxes are necessary, a capital tax is useless; in depression, when capital taxes would be useful, they are not necessary. This is the reason why they are so little used.

The only really acceptable form of capital tax is the Death Duty. It is doubtful whether death duties have much effect in dissuading people from saving during their lifetime, though they may encourage 'gifts *inter vivos*' intended to avoid the tax. It is certainly hard for economists to make reasonable assumptions about how people will react to a tax that is only levied after they are dead. Nor does it seem probable that death duties will, in general, have any significant effects on the savings habits of heirs.

Progressive death duties do, however, serve an important purpose. They probably have little effect on a man's incentive to work and save during his lifetime, and yet they do help to make the distribution of incomes more equal. One of the most reliable ways of ensuring that a man has an extremely high income is to leave him a fortune which he can invest in securities which will yield him a high 'unearned' income for the rest of his life. It seems almost certain that the best way of reducing the inequality of incomes is to make it certain that one can only become rich by one's own efforts during one's lifetime. This is what death duties do. Moreover, many people who think that it is wrong to prevent people, by income taxes, from enjoying the fruits of their labours during their lifetime, would be quite willing to see everyone start life in much the same financial position—by the imposition of high taxes on bequests.

High death duties do, however, suffer from one major defect. They make it less easy for industry to borrow money from private investors. For example, it is the big investment institutions—insurance companies, the Ecclesiastical Commission, and so on—who are becoming the really big 'capitalists' in post-war Britain. Because of high death duties, the 'millionaire' capitalist has almost disappeared from this country. This need not necessarily be a bad thing; but its implications, in terms of the distribution of economic and also political power, could be very important. Again, the disappearance of the 'capitalist' in the old-fashioned sense may mean that the organisation of the capital market has to change. If the country's supply of capital is in future to come from the 'small saver', new ways of enabling people to lend their money to industry may become necessary. The present organisation of the London Stock Exchange, for example, may not be ideal for attracting the savings of the working-man or the capital of widows and orphans.

CHAPTER XI

INTERNATIONAL TRADE

THIS book has been concerned so far with a study of the 'closed' economy and has ignored international trade. We have seen that the problems of such 'closed' economies are by no means simple to understand. But there is probably much less understanding of the problems of international trade than of internal economic problems. This is partly because the ordinary man seems to regard the complexities of international trade and of foreign currencies as unusually mysterious phenomena. It is probably also partly as a result of the difficulties of the post-war international economy. The lack of balance in the trade between the United States and many other countries in the world; devaluation; exchange controls; import restrictions—all these things have led to much uncertainty and confusion about the true nature of international trade.

It is therefore important to realise that there is no separate economic theory of international trade. All its features can be explained in terms of the kind of economic theory that has been outlined so far in this book. In particular, international trade is an example of a fundamental economic phenomenon discussed earlier—the division of labour.

Trade takes place between different countries because consumers, firms, and sometimes Governments, exchange goods across political frontiers for the same kind of reasons as they exchange goods within a single country. We are so used to the modern society where the division of labour is one of the most noticeable features, that we tend to take this division of labour for granted; yet we do not accept it so readily in the sphere of international trade. Within any country, farmers, motor-car manufacturers and railway workers concentrate their attention on their own particular jobs, thus becoming efficient and expert in these occupations and enabling the community to achieve a high standard of living. Similarly, the standard of living of the world as a whole benefits from the fact that countries specialise in particular fields of activity. Britain is predominantly an industrial country; New Zealand concentrates on agriculture. Again, Switzerland produces no motor-cars. Her industry specialises on the production of heavy trucks suited to her severe road system; all her motor-cars are imported. A time-honoured instance of international economic specialisation is that, whilst it would doubtless be possible to grow grapes on a large scale in Scotland in greenhouses, the Scots wisely leave the large-scale production of grapes to countries like Italy where they can be grown in the open air, and therefore more cheaply.

Where, as in such cases, one country has an obvious technical or natural advantage in a particular field, the ultimate value of specialisation is obvious. The world as a whole reaps benefits if the 'absolute advantages' possessed by particular countries are exploited to the full. But international trade will still be beneficial where countries have what are called *comparative advantages* as opposed to these absolute advantages just studied.

Comparative advantages explain why trade takes place between rich, efficient countries and poor countries. For example, it is almost certain that Britain could produce some agricultural products more efficiently than the countries from whom she buys them. But it is more beneficial for Britons that they should concentrate their attention on producing engineering goods which can then be exchanged for the agricultural products in question. For whilst Britain may be a more efficient producer of such agricultural products than the country in question, her productive efficiency gives her an even greater advantage in engineering; her *comparative advantage* is greater in engineering than in agriculture.

To put the point somewhat ungrammatically, all countries benefit if Britain concentrates on the production of those goods at whose production she is 'most best' and the other countries specialise on those lines in which they are 'least worst'. In this way all countries benefit from the international division of labour. At least, this is the long-established contention of economists. The only doubt arises from the difficulty of producing a convincing example from real life. In a world of tariffs and quotas, exchange control and government regulations, it is hard for the economist to be sure how valid such 'toy' examples really are.

Specialisation based on *comparative* advantages does, of course, occur within the individual country. Most professional musicians could teach their own children to play the piano more successfully than anyone else could, at any rate whilst the children were young. But it will pay them to spend the time which would have been needed to teach their children in earning professional fees, and to pay someone else to give their children music lessons. Similarly, most women doctors would be better able to do their own housework than any hired woman. But they find it more lucrative (as well as more satisfying) to spend their time on doctoring, where their 'comparative advantage' is greatest, and to pay someone else to do the housework—albeit not so efficiently as they could have done it themselves.

Such, then, is the basis of international trade. Both the individual countries, and the world as a whole, will attain a higher standard of living if specialisation is allowed to develop in the way outlined above. It is for this reason that the idea of completely free and unrestricted international trade has always been popular with economists. Where trade is completely free and untrammelled, the anxiety of business men to buy in the cheapest markets and to engage in the most lucrative occupations will lead to exactly the pattern of specialisation that has been outlined above. It was, for example, the establishment of Free Trade in Britain about the middle of the nineteenth century which led her to turn from farming to become 'the workshop of the world'. Similarly, it was only as a result of the abandonment of free trade in agricultural products that British agriculture revived during the 1930's and 1940's.

Although there is no separate theory of international trade, the subject attracts special interest because of its close connection with economic welfare—especially in countries like Britain, where trade plays such a vital part in economic affairs. There is, for example, much modern scepticism both about the practicability of free trade in the unsettled world of today and about the assumptions underlying the theory outlined above.

Two main criticisms of the assumptions can be made. First, as we have seen, there is some doubt whether it is possible to find many instances of countries specialising in the production of given commodities because they possess comparative, but not absolute, advantages in these particular fields. For example, one might suppose that the fact that Britain exports motor-cars to the United States, which herself makes such cars, proves that Britain possesses a comparative advantage in the production of motor-cars. Yet, in fact, one suspects that these exports occur because there is no single homogeneous good called a motor-car. There are many different types; and those which Britain exports to America probably have distinct advantages to the purchaser in the United States over American cars. The man who wants the unique craftsmanship of Rolls Royce can find nothing to satisfy him that is made in America. The man who wants a tiny sports car cannot do so either. In other words, when one studies what are, on the face of it, instances of specialisation based on comparative advantages in a general market, it usually appears that they are really instances of the country in question possessing *absolute* productive advantages in some small and special sectors of that general market. It is therefore difficult to convince oneself that very much of the world's trade today is based on *comparative* cost advantages.

A second doubt arises over the idea that a country can possess a *long-term* advantage in the production of any given product, except with some primary products whose efficient production depends on geographical factors. For example, Britain's supremacy in textiles during the nineteenth century has been stolen by newcomers in countries like India and Japan. It is only with agricultural products where a country's climatic advantage cannot be taken away, or with the possession of valuable mineral deposits that long-term productive advantages seem likely to exist.

Such doubts, reinforced by the many difficulties of the unsettled world economy between 1914 and the present day, have led many people to wonder whether there really is a complete case for free trade. In fact, the general case for free trade remains as strong as ever; but three qualifications to it are now widely accepted.

First, it is agreed that there may be a case for imposing a tariff on the import of goods which compete with the output of a new and growing industry. The tariff will raise the price of imported products but will leave the price of home-produced goods unaffected, thereby strengthening the growing industry's competitive position. So, the argument runs, the 'infant industry' will be able to grow to maturity, a thing which would never have happened if the tariff had not been imposed on the products of its foreign rivals. The only objection to such a procedure is that any such tariff, once imposed, tends to be very difficult to remove. The 'infant', when it has reached maturity, will not often display any great enthusiasm for abandoning the supports which have enabled it to grow. It will be so much easier to carry on as before.

The second case in which tariffs may be thought desirable is where they are used to foster the growth of industries that are essential to defence. Thus, since the early 1920's, Britain has supported the production of scientific instruments by a tariff in order that she should not in future depend on foreign instruments in time of war. This 'strategic' argument for tariffs is clearly a forceful one in an insecure world, where military security is preferred to economic welfare.

Finally, it is usually agreed that long-term planning in agriculture may be impossible unless there is a tariff to keep out cheaper foreign imports, raise home prices, and allow farmers to bring 'marginal land' profitably into cultivation. Only in this way can a long-term plan for increased self-sufficiency be carried out. Such self-sufficiency is sometimes regarded as desirable in itself, again mainly as a result of the desire to ensure food supplies in time of war.

It is worth noting here that whilst we have implied that tariffs are the most likely method of protection, they are not necessarily the only method. A tariff, by raising the price of imports, will improve the competitive position of home producers. But the effects of a tariff on the *quantity* of imports cannot often be accurately predicted. For this effect will depend on the supply and demand conditions for the imported goods. It follows that where a country wishes to be certain exactly how much of a given product will be imported during any period of time, it will impose a 'quota' system. Under this, once the given 'quota' of imports has been allowed into the country in a given period of time, no further imports at all will be allowed until the next 'quota period' begins.

It must be pointed out finally, however, that nothing that has been said above is intended to suggest that the imposition of a tariff is a desirable way of increasing the level of employment in a country. It is possible that restrictions on the import of, say, wheat, may increase employment among home producers of wheat. But the foreign country which previously supplied that wheat will now suffer a decline in its exports; it may retaliate by imposing tariffs against the first country's exports. If it does, a progressive tariff 'war' will start, at the end of which employment in the world as a whole may well be lower than at the beginning. And even if the level of employment does not fall, standards of living will. The cure for unemployment is not to raise tariff barriers. The kind of full employment policy outlined earlier should be followed. In addition, steps should be taken to move workers out of any industry that has become inefficient compared with the industries of other countries, and into more promising lines of production.

CHAPTER XII

FOREIGN EXCHANGE RATES

ALTHOUGH there is no separate theory of international trade, international economic problems become significantly different from those *within* an economy, once we allow for the fact that each country has its own banking system. One can see this clearly if one considers the problems of the 'depressed area' of South Wales during the slump of the early 1930's. Unemployment in this area was extremely high because the demand for the area's main products, coal and iron and steel goods, collapsed. It seems fairly certain that even the relatively low standard of living that was sustained in South Wales in the 1930's must have been maintained to a large degree by unemployment benefits and other relief payments made by the British Central Government out of general national funds. If South Wales had been a separate country, very difficult problems would have arisen. South Wales would almost certainly have faced a serious 'sterling shortage'. She would have been hard pressed to earn enough sterling to pay for essential foodstuffs. Thus, even if the 'South Wales Government' had been willing to run a budget deficit, in order to pay unemployment benefits, there would have been difficulty in turning these money receipts into goods. For the goods themselves would have needed to be imported, and 'foreign currency' would have been short.

This is the kind of problem which arises whenever different countries each have their own monetary authority and money supply. The problems of a separate 'South Wales' in the 1930's could not have been solved by purely 'internal' monetary policy. The same kind of assistance as was in fact received from the British Government would still have been necessary to maintain any kind of living standards at all. But it would now have needed a 'sterling loan' paid by the British Government to the 'South Wales Government'. And it is much easier to persuade one's own Government to pay unemployment benefits to all its own subjects than it is to obtain a loan for 'foreigners'. The existence of different nations and different banking and monetary systems therefore raises many financial problems which would not exist, even if the underlying purely economic problems were exactly the same, where there was only one Government, one monetary authority and a real community of interest between all peoples.

The first and most obvious result of the existence of different kinds of money in different countries is that each of these currencies has a 'price' in terms of each other. Thus a pound note can be bought for, say, three dollars or twelve Swiss francs. One Swiss franc costs a hundred French francs, and so on. A whole new set of prices, or 'foreign exchange rates' arises, and a new world-wide market—the foreign exchange market—has to exist to deal in them. This chapter will explain what determines foreign exchange rates and why, say, Swiss francs are dearer in terms of pounds at some times than at others.

Inevitably, this is a problem of demand and supply. Swiss francs cost more in terms of pounds when the demand for Swiss francs is great and the supply of them is small; they cost less when the supply of Swiss francs is great and the demand for them is small. And the demand for Swiss francs is exactly the same thing as the supply of the other currencies—pounds, dollars, etc. —which people are offering in exchange for them. The demand for any currency is the supply of the others which people are giving in exchange for it.

Let us now see what are the main reasons why people will demand any given currency, say pounds. First, there will be demands arising from the kind of commodity trade discussed in the previous chapter. Individuals and firms in other countries will wish to buy those goods in whose production Britain has advantages. They will pay for these exports from Britain by supplying their own currencies, and will therefore create a demand for pounds. Similarly, of course, firms and individuals in Britain will wish to buy the produce of foreign countries. And the pounds which are paid for such imports into Britain will represent a supply of pounds sterling on the foreign exchange market.

The second main type of transaction which will give rise to the demand and supply of sterling on the foreign exchange market will be what are known as 'invisible' imports and exports. Just as the 'visible' import and export of physical goods will mean that there is 'visible' trade between countries, so there will be 'invisible' trade in services like shipping, insurance and banking. Foreigners will wish to make use of the facilities offered by British insurance companies; they will wish to have their goods transported in British ships; and they will wish to avail themselves of the banking services provided by the 'City' of London. Such 'invisible' exports will represent a source of income to Britain just as much as will the export of actual 'visible' goods like tractors or textiles. Like these visible exports, the 'invisibles' will also create a demand for sterling. Foreigners will supply their own currencies on the foreign exchange market and will thus create a demand for pounds.

British people and firms will also wish to make use of the 'invisible' services afforded by other countries. Such 'invisible' imports will obviously have to be paid for, and this will result in a supply of sterling on the foreign exchange market.

Third, at various times in the past, most countries will, through individuals or firms, have lent money to people or firms in other countries. A further important 'invisible' trade item will therefore be the interest payments on such money as has been lent abroad or borrowed from abroad. Interest payments made *to* Britain, interest on her past overseas investments, will create a demand for sterling. Those people in foreign countries who are making the interest payments will only possess their own currencies and will therefore demand sterling. For it is sterling which the British nationals who own the overseas investments will wish to receive. Similarly, where it is foreigners who have previously invested their money in Britain, interest payments will be made *by* Britain, and these will represent a supply of sterling on the foreign exchange market to be exchanged for the appropriate foreign currencies.

It is a short step from discussing such interest payments to considering, fourth, the investment on which they depend. International investment can take two forms. It can mean that individuals or groups of people in one country carry out acts of *real* investment by building, say, railways, factories or harbours in other countries. Or it can take the form of long-term 'money investment' where people in one country purchase long-term securities issued in other countries.

Where overseas investment takes the form of the purchase of foreign securities, demands and supplies of foreign currencies will arise in the same kind of ways as with visible or invisible trade. Where foreigners lend money to Britain it is as though British securities have been 'exported' to them. The foreigners will pay some of their own currencies to those in Britain who are issuing long-term securities; these foreign currencies will constitute a demand for sterling. Similarly the sterling paid by Britons who are 'importing' overseas securities will constitute a supply of sterling on the foreign exchange market.

Where *real* overseas investment is being financed by Britain, this finance can take two forms. First it may be that the sterling subscribed by British investors will be used to buy foreign currencies, and that these currencies will then be used to buy raw materials and hire indigenous labour in the countries where the investment project is being carried out. In this case, there will be a supply of sterling on the foreign exchange market in exchange for the foreign currencies in question. Conversely, of course, any *real* foreign investment in Britain will lead to a demand for sterling. Foreigners who have built up, say, dollar funds to finance an investment project in Britain will wish to exchange them for pounds in order to pay British constructional labour, and so on.

The second way of financing *real* investment overseas is for the investing country, say Britain, both to provide the actual physical equipment needed and also to lend the foreign country the sterling to pay for these goods. Here there is what may be called a 'tied loan', where the lending country provides the borrower with money to be spent on the lender's own products. Such loans are by no means unknown in Britain. For example, during the nineteenth century Britain supplied almost the whole world with railways; and she lent out the money to pay for them. In such a case, there would be a demand for, say, sterling from the country which was receiving the investment; this would be matched by an exactly equal supply of sterling from the British lenders who were providing the finance.

Similar instances have occurred since 1945. Many countries lent money to Britain to help to finance the war. These loans were known as 'sterling balances' held in London. After the war had ended, such countries were allowed to 'run down' their accumulated 'sterling balances' by buying British goods. These 'unrequited exports' were not balanced by any import of physical goods; again Britain 'lent' the money to pay for them by repaying her war-time debts.

We have carefully distinguished these two ways of financing real investment overseas. In practice many foreign loans will represent a combination of these two kinds. Some of the money lent will be spent on the produce of the lending country; some will be turned into the currency of the receiving country and spent there.

Similar long-term international capital movements will occur when there is a 'flight of capital' from one country to another. If, for some reason, people become convinced that the long-term economic and political future of a given country is a bleak one, they may well decide to sell the securities which they hold in that country, and transfer their capital to places where they think the outlook is brighter. Such capital movements will represent a supply of the currency from which the 'flight' is occurring and a demand for the currency of the country to which the funds are being transferred. Capital 'fleeing' from Britain would increase the supply of sterling on the foreign exchange market; a flight towards Britain would raise the demand for sterling.

Clearly such capital movements can be on an extremely large scale; they may easily dwarf the normal day-by-day transactions which are occurring on the foreign exchange market. A sudden inflow of capital to a country often causes so great an increase in the demand for its currency that there is a substantial, though probably quite short-lived, rise in the foreign exchange value of that currency. Similarly, an outflow of capital can, for a short period of time, cause a catastrophic fall in the foreign exchange value of a country's currency.

Just as there will be such long-term 'money investment' of capital in different countries, so there will be short-term lending and borrowing, where short-term rates of interest in one country are more favourable than in another. For example, after the end of the war, short-term rates of interest were higher in Belgium than in Britain. British banks with funds available for short-term lending therefore tended to transfer some of their funds to Belgium, where this was possible, in order to obtain the higher return available there. Similarly, during the summer of 1954 short-term interest rates were higher in Britain than in Switzerland, and short-term funds were moved temporarily from Zürich to London in search of higher returns, creating a short-lived demand for sterling.

A fifth reason why foreigners will demand, say, sterling, is that they may wish to 'hoard' it. They may want to hold sterling, whether it yields them interest payments or not, merely because

they feel that there are likely to be short-term advantages from
holding sterling. The main reason will be that they think that
sterling is likely to become more valuable in terms of given
foreign currencies. A Frenchman, for example, may fear that
the franc is about to be devalued. He will therefore wish to hold
sterling temporarily, in order to make a capital profit by con-
verting the sterling back into francs once devaluation has taken
place and the franc is 'cheaper' in terms of sterling than it was
before. It should be noted, however, that the movement of
'hoards' of money does not here imply the movement of actual
physical 'cash'. It merely means that the ownership of bank
balances changes, Frenchmen 'buying' bank balances in London,
and so on.

Movements of such money 'hoards' from one country to
another have been quite common during the past few decades
when both the normal workings of the market, and deliberate
acts of devaluation by Governments, have led to substantial and
sudden changes in the values of many currencies. Money which
moves from one country to another in search of such quick
'speculative' gains is known as 'hot' money. It rarely stays in
one place for long; and it has the disadvantage that by its very
movement it will tend to strengthen and perpetuate any short-
term change in the foreign exchange value of a currency.

For example, if sterling shows signs of appreciating in terms
of other currencies, this may lead to expectations of a further rise
in the value of sterling. Consequently, there will be an inflow
of 'hot' money to London. This short-term inflow will in itself
lead to a further rise in the foreign exchange value of sterling
and this will further swell the inward movement of 'hot' money.
In other words, the process feeds on itself.

The sixth main source of the demand for any country's
currency lies in the transactions of Governments. These can be
divided into two types. First, there is expenditure undertaken
independently of the foreign exchange value of a country's
currency. Both expenditure incurred in keeping armies in other
countries, and also outright gifts to a foreign government, will
create a supply of the paying Government's currency on the
foreign exchange market. It will represent a demand for the
recipient's currency.

Perhaps more important in the present context, however, will
be expenditure by a Government which is deliberately intended
to influence the foreign exchange value of its currency. If the

'price' of, say, sterling is temporarily high, the British Government may (through the Bank of England) decide to keep the exchange rate of sterling down. It will do this by buying up amounts of other countries' currencies, thereby deliberately increasing the *supply* of sterling on the foreign exchange market. The stocks of foreign currencies so acquired can be spent later, if sterling becomes too 'cheap', to increase the *demand* for sterling on the foreign exchange market thereby raising its 'price'. In such a way, the foreign exchange value of any country's currency can be kept much more stable than the uncontrolled operation of market forces would allow.

We have now seen the main factors on which the demands and supplies of any currency on the foreign exchange market will depend. We now consider the underlying economic forces which will influence the size of such demands and supplies, and thereby determine the actual foreign exchange value of a currency.

Let us first consider the factors influencing the demands and supplies for a currency that arise in the normal course of 'visible' and 'invisible' trade. Such trade will be largely unaffected by short-term phenomena like the movement of 'hot' money. More than this, the demands and supplies of currencies arising from such trade, and hence foreign exchange rates also, must depend ultimately on the costs of production in the various countries. If costs of production in any country are high, the demand for its visible and invisible exports will fall off; at the same time its own inhabitants will wish to buy the cheaper products of the foreign countries, with their lower costs of production. The demand for the high-cost country's currency on the foreign exchange market will fall and the supply of it will rise, thereby lowering the foreign exchange value of the country's currency. This process will continue until the falling foreign exchange value of the 'high-cost' country's currency brings its own export prices into line with the domestic prices of other countries in the world.

Perhaps, before going any further, it will be worth while to give an illustration of the way in which such fall in the foreign exchange value of a country's currency can bring its export costs and prices—and hence the demands and supplies for its currency —into line with prices and costs in the rest of the world.

Let us assume that an American car costs $1200 and a British car £300. If the rate of exchange is £1 = $3, a Briton will have to pay £300 for a British car, but £400 for an American one. Similarly, an American will have to pay $1200 for a car made in his own country, but only $900 for a British car. The tendency will therefore be for British cars to be bought by *both* the British and the Americans; British cars are cheaper. This tendency will lead to a decline in the demand for dollars by Britons buying American cars, and, at the same time, to an increase in the supply of dollars from Americans buying British cars. The result will be to lower the foreign exchange value of the dollar (raise that of the pound) until, with a rate of exchange of £1 = $4, a car costs £300 (or $1200) in both countries. This illustration shows that where production costs and prices in various countries are out of line, a 'depreciation' in the exchange value of the high-cost country's currency will bring about an equalisation of export prices throughout the world.

It is therefore only natural that economists should have developed a theory which explains the fundamental connection between foreign exchange rates and the levels of costs and prices in the various countries. This is the 'purchasing power parity' theory. It shows that, in the long run, when short-period capital movements can be ignored, the 'normal' rate of exchange between two currencies will depend on the general level of prices in the two countries. More precisely, the 'purchasing-power parity' theory asserts that, ignoring all capital movements, long- or short-period, the rate of exchange in a completely uncontrolled market will settle automatically at a level where the purchasing power of the two currencies is the same. If a country has a high internal price level, its currency will have a low purchasing power internally and a low foreign exchange value externally. In other words, a currency's internal and external purchasing power will both move in step.

The purchasing power parity theory is important because it throws light on the vital and fundamental link between internal price levels and the external value of currencies. It shows why inflation within a country so often goes together with a sagging price for its currency on the foreign exchange market. It also shows, for example, that the long-run answer to the competition of low-cost 'sweated' labour lies not in the imposition of tariffs or quotas on imports into the 'high cost' country, but in the certainty that the automatic operation of market forces will raise the foreign exchange rate against such 'low-cost' producers. The very success of, say, the Japanese in exporting will increase the demand for their currency—and hence the yen will appreciate. The yen will cost more in terms of pounds or dollars than before.

K

There are, however, two qualifications to the purchasing-power parity theory. First, as we have seen, it relates only to the foreign exchange rates that arise through the exchange of goods and services; it abstracts entirely from the short-run (and even the long-run) effects of capital movements. Capital movements cannot easily be related to the underlying costs of production. This is why we have described the purchasing-power parity theory as explaining long-run 'normal' levels of exchange rates, those which will be reached when the influence of capital movements is at its least.

A second reservation to this theory is that it will provide a better explanation of exchange rates where the greater part of a country's exports are subject to free international trade. A tariff, by preventing free and widespread trade, may mean that foreign exchange rates do not bear any close relationship to the domestic purchasing power of the various currencies. Again, if goods are sold only in a local market, as are, for example, hair-cuts, there may be little relation between the prices of such goods and foreign exchange rates. They will not enter at all into world trade. Despite these minor qualifications, the purchasing power parity theory has held its ground for several decades. It is the best and most general explanation of the way in which visible and invisible trade in goods and services influences the demands and supplies of currencies, and thus their foreign exchange values.

If we turn to long-term international investment, we find that, like domestic investment, it depends mainly on expected rates of return. The business man wishing to build a new factory may consider not only the rate of return which he will receive in his own country; he may also consider the prospective yields elsewhere in the world.

Much international movement of capital takes place because business men, private individuals and firms, which are seeking to purchase equities, will decide to make their 'money' or their 'real' investments in countries where the expected rate of return is higher than it is at home. New and developing countries, like Australia, attract 'real' and 'money' investment from older countries like Britain. The expected rates of return in these as yet 'under-developed' countries are sufficiently tempting to attract capital from other countries. Thus, where the expected rate of return on investment in a country is high, there will be much demand for that country's currency from people who wish to make long-term investments in it. This is perhaps the main reason for long-term international investment—the desire to 'cash in' on the high rates of return earned by investment in 'new' countries. It is also possible that there may be some long-term investment in such countries—and hence demands for their currencies—because rates of interest on long-term bonds (as opposed to equities) are higher abroad than at home. But it does not seem easy to discover any very close connection between high long-term rates of interest, say, on Government bonds, and the state of economic development in a country. Rates of interest, as opposed to equity dividends, may depend on factors that are neither fundamental nor predictable, such as the policy of a country's monetary authorities.

The rate of interest does, however, play a major rôle in causing short-term movements of capital from one country to another, as we have already seen. This leads us to consider what has, traditionally, been perhaps the most important rôle of 'Bank Rate'. We have seen that economists in discussing monetary policy are nowadays inclined to regard Bank Rate as of little account. But in the past, especially when the 'Gold Standard' still lasted, a rise in Bank Rate played a vitally important rôle in attracting short-term funds towards a country which was losing its gold because of a balance of payments deficit. A rise in short-term interest rates rapidly and effectively attracted short-term loans to the country, and allowed a 'breathing space' during which a more permanent remedy could be found.

Before 1914, therefore, the British monetary authorities relied heavily on changes in Bank Rate as a way of safeguarding the country's gold reserves. A rise in Bank Rate acted as a signal to both home and foreign banks that interest rates in Britain ought to, and would, rise. Indeed, during the period of the 'Gold Standard', the short-term rate of interest seems to have represented a mechanism that was both delicate and effective. It encouraged foreign lending to the country which had instituted a 'dear money' policy, halting any outflow of gold. Thus there grew up the nineteenth-century saying, 'Seven per cent will draw gold from the moon!'

Such continual reliance on the rate of interest to control the inflow and outflow of short-term funds is not now common. Yet as the world moves away from the dislocation of the immediate post-war years, there may well be a greater use of short-term interest rates as a way of controlling what is considered to be excessively large inflow or outflow of funds. For example,

we have already seen that in 1954 there was an inflow of funds
to London, based largely on the fact that short-term interest
rates were higher in London than in Zürich. The British Government's immediate reaction was to lower Bank Rate—as a sign
that interest rates in London were too high. This was the traditional response to an excessive inflow of short-term funds.

We have seen that the main reason for the movement of
'hoards' of 'hot' money is the expectation that particular currencies will be devalued. People, and more especially banks,
with surplus funds, switch their resources from the 'soft' to the
'hard' currencies, for they know that the latter are unlikely to
be devalued. Such people can be justly described as 'specu-
lators', they are gambling on their conviction that devaluation
of 'soft' currencies is likely.

Now it is, of course, possible that businesses and banks will
behave in a similar way when they make normal everyday payments for goods and services. For example, at various dates
between 1945 and 1951 American business-men became convinced
that a devaluation of the pound was likely; certainly they felt
that a *rise* in the foreign exchange value of the pound was quite
out of the question. At such times, American business-men held
back their dollar payments to Britain until the last possible
moment, knowing that by doing so they could not lose; and
they might well gain if the value of sterling fell—that is, if the
number of dollars needed to buy each pound decreased. British
business-men took the same view of the situation, and when they
bought American goods, paid at the *earliest* possible moment,
thereby forestalling any devaluation of the pound. For devaluation would mean that an increased number of pounds would be
needed to buy a given number of dollars.

'Pressure' on the pound, then, can develop not only from the
movement of 'hoards' of money—held by individuals, and firms
indulging in pure speculation. It can come, too, from the holding
back of perfectly normal business purchases of a currency by
foreign traders who think it will be devalued, reinforced by the
enthusiasm of those within the devaluing country to make their
own payments to other countries as rapidly as possible, and for
the same reason. This speeding up and slowing down of payments can represent an important source of changed foreign
exchange rates. For it will lower the demand and raise the supply
of the suspect currency and therefore help to lower its 'price'.
Such speeding up and slowing down of payments may even *force*

devaluation of a currency if it sufficiently lowers confidence in that currency.

It is to help all business-men who do not wish to take risks over the future level of foreign exchange rates that the 'forward exchange market' exists. Its function is to enable business men to avoid having to run any such risks over foreign exchange rates, by allowing them to 'cover' their future transactions. The process is simple. Suppose that a British trader agrees to buy goods worth $1000 from America in three months' time. If he is unwilling to 'gamble' on the sterling foreign exchange rate remaining favourable, he will ask his bank to sell him the necessary dollars for delivery in three months' time—he buys the dollars 'forward'. Now banks do not 'gamble' by hoping that the sterling-dollar exchange rate in three months' time will have become more favourable to them than it is now; such 'gambling' is barred to British banks. The British bank will therefore 'cover its position'. It will buy the dollars *now*—'on the spot', as it is said. These 'spot' dollars will be invested in short-term securities in New York until, in three months' time, they will be delivered to the British importer, or, more probably, directly to his American supplier. In this way both the British importer and the British banker are 'covered' against loss.

This type of 'forward' transaction represents the kind of service that is provided by the forward exchange market. It enables both business-men and banks to avoid risks. It also means that unless business-men are *almost certain* that devaluation of a currency is coming, few, if any, business-men will 'speculate' by 'hoarding' the stronger currency until the last possible moment. As we have seen, such speeding up and slowing down of purchases is important at times; but there are only fairly narrow limits within which the date of payment can be altered. Few business transactions allow much more than three months from the initial order to the final payment.

The existence of the forward exchange market therefore means that foreign exchange deals made in the normal course of business rarely lead to the movement of 'hoards' of money. And a 'forward exchange' transaction is really a form of short-term investment. The British bank which 'covers' its position by holding dollars in New York for later payment to its client is 'investing' short-term funds. This has an obvious consequence. The price at which 'forward' currencies can be bought will depend on the short-term rates of interest in the countries in question.

For example, suppose that short-term interest rates are higher in New York than in London. The British customer who asks his banker to buy dollars on his behalf and hold them in New York for three months, is, in fact, doing his banker a good turn. By giving the bank a sound reason for buying dollars now, the customer will have enabled the bank to earn a higher rate of interest on its money than it would have done if that money had stayed in London. The bank will allow the customer to share in its good fortune by charging a slightly lower price for 'forward' dollars than it has itself paid for 'spot' dollars. This means that forward dollars are 'at a discount'.

Conversely, of course, if the rate of interest is lower in New York than in London, 'forward' dollars will be dearer than they are 'on the spot'—they will be 'at a premium'. The customer will then have to recompense his banker for the fact that the latter has money on loan in New York which could have earned him a higher rate of interest in London. The customer therefore has to pay more for 'forward' dollars than his banker paid for 'spot' dollars. It follows that the size of any discount or premium on the 'forward' price of a given foreign currency depends on short-term rates of interest in the countries concerned.

The movement of currency 'hoards', or 'uncovered' balances, cannot arise from the operations of the forward exchange market. It is only where people *refrain* from using the foreign exchange market to 'cover their position' that speculative 'hoards' are held. Such 'hoards' will sometimes be held by individuals and firms who feel that any money capital they have will be most profitably employed in 'speculating' on the devaluation of some particular currency. In the present-day world, however, perhaps the most important 'speculative hoards' are those held by Central Banks. As we have seen, the British commercial banks do not 'gamble' by 'hoarding' foreign currencies; they will always 'cover' their positions. Central Banks, however, will be prepared to 'hold positions' in foreign currencies. Central Banks will not always 'cover their positions' but will hold the foreign currencies, which they acquire in their normal transactions, in whatever currency seems most appropriate. It is therefore the world's Central Banks that probably hold the most important 'speculative hoards' of foreign currencies at present.

This leads us to our final point. What determines the Governments' demands and supplies of different currencies? First, there will be the demands for and supplies of its own currency which arise because a Government wishes to maintain the foreign exchange value of that currency at a stable level. The way in which such a policy will operate can be seen if we study the British 'Exchange Equalisation Account' which was set up in 1932, after the 'Gold Standard' had finally been abandoned. The main aim of the Exchange Equalisation Account is to cancel out fluctuations in foreign exchange rates which are a result of purely short-term factors. It cannot be expected that the receipts and payments of any country will balance every day, or even every week. There is no reason why the transactions carried out by two different countries in any short period of time should balance exactly.

The same is true of seasonal factors. It is inevitable that countries have to buy particular goods at certain times of the year. Where the goods are agricultural products, the periods of peak trade will obviously be influenced by the time of harvest. But even manufactured goods, for example clothing, have their peak seasons; and it would be unwise to expect the different seasonal factors affecting any given country's trade to cancel each other out at any given moment. Seasonal factors therefore cause short-term fluctuations in exchange rates. It is clearly in the interest of healthy trading conditions that such fluctuations should be ironed out whenever possible. They are not the result of fundamental differences between economic conditions in the countries concerned, and which, if they did exist, ought to be allowed to give rise to changes in exchange rates. They are caused purely and simply by short-term and transient factors which have no fundamental or lasting economic significance.

At the time when the British Exchange Equalisation Account was set up, there was another more serious cause of temporary fluctuations in the exchange rate. Political and economic conditions in the early 1930's were extremely unstable, and there was a considerable movement of funds from country to country in search of a safe resting-place. Such money might flow into a country to the tune of several hundred million pounds at one moment, and flow out again within six months. Clearly, these large sums could have an enormous effect on the balance of payments and exchange rate of the receiving and the losing countries. Yet the movement of such 'hot' money did not indicate the existence of any fundamental economic disequilibrium; and it was felt desirable that its effect on the foreign exchange rate should be kept as small as possible.

The Exchange Equalisation Account is not concerned with attempting to offset the effects of any of the more fundamental forces which may cause balance of payment difficulties. Apart from the obvious difficulty of attempting to offset any fundamental economic change by Government action, it was no purpose of the fund to do so. Long-term changes in the nature of world economy can only work out their very necessary effects if they are allowed to exert their influence on foreign exchange rates.

We must now consider the way in which the Exchange Equalisation Account has carried out its aim of preventing short-term differences between payments and receipts, and also movements of 'hot' money, from exerting their normal effect on the balance of payments. Briefly, when exports temporarily exceed imports, or when there is an inward movement of foreign capital, the exchange rate tends to rise. The demand for pounds tends to outrun the supply. The 'Account' will therefore buy up some of the incoming foreign currency, or gold, whichever it happens to be, and which is causing the value of the pound to rise on the foreign exchange market. If the 'Account' buys sufficient gold and foreign currency, it will be able to keep the rate down to its old level. The Account, in other words, increases the supply of pounds on the foreign exchange market. The result of this transaction is to provide the Account with a store of gold and foreign currency which can be used later to prevent any future fall in the rate. If imports exceed exports, or 'hot' money flows out, the supply of pounds will exceed the demand. The Account will then step in and buy up the pounds with its stocks of gold and currency. This will prevent the exchange rate from falling.

It is clear that serious problems would arise if the Exchange Equalisation Account *were* used in any attempt to maintain the foreign exchange rate of the pound in the face of a fundamental balance of payments disequilibrium. If, in such circumstances, an attempt were made to prevent the pound's foreign exchange value from falling, the Account's reserves of gold and currency would be depleted and would ultimately run out. On the other hand, it would be rather easier to meet a permanent *excess* of the foreign demand for sterling over the supply of sterling at the current exchange rate. The Account would merely have to continue to buy up all the gold and foreign currency offered, thereby piling up stocks of gold. The only real embarrassment of such a policy would be the problem of storing away the gold without allowing it to affect the internal monetary system—a problem not unheard of in the U.S.A.

The rest of the Government's foreign exchange transactions will arise from expenditure that bears no close relation to the foreign exchange rate. In the recent past, much of such expenditure has been devoted to maintaining armies overseas, which has led to a demand for the currency of the country where the troops were stationed. More recently, however, there has been a growing tendency for Western Governments to spend money on relieving poverty and distress in the 'underdeveloped areas' of the world. This creates a demand for the currencies of the 'underdeveloped areas'. These countries do not represent attractive fields for business investment. Poverty means that the prospective yields of any investments are extremely low, and the underlying political uncertainties are great. Yet the *need* for investment is overwhelming. It is only Governments, attracted by other than purely business motives, which can help here.

It may be, therefore, that the 'Colombo Plan', whereby Britain, America and other countries are granting assistance to non-Communist South-East Asia, may become a pattern for the future. Government expenditure in the foreign exchange market during the second half of the twentieth century may well be typified by the giving of help to the 'backward countries' of the world. Some of this help may be mobilised and organised by the World Bank for Reconstruction and Development, set up at the end of the war to perform just such a task; and help of this kind will represent a supply of pounds or dollars on the foreign exchange markets of the world in exchange for the currencies of 'backward' areas.

CHAPTER XIII

THE BALANCE OF PAYMENTS

WE have seen how the demands and supplies, and therefore the price, of a country's currency will be determined on the foreign exchange market. The 'external price' of its currency is, however, not the only thing which will concern the government of a country. For this 'price' is, so to speak, only a visible indicator, showing whether the demands and supplies of the country's currency are in balance on the foreign exchange market. In order to understand the reasons for any change in the foreign exchange value of its own currency, and, even more important, to cure or even forestall a change in this foreign exchange rate, a government will find it essential to know what are the *amounts* of its currency which are currently being demanded and supplied. The usual way of showing any country's international financial position is to draw up its 'Balance of Payments'. This is, in effect, the balance-sheet of the country's international transactions, and it shows all the receipts from and payments to the rest of the world during a given period of time, usually a year.

Let us, for the moment, assume that there are only two countries in the 'world', Britain and America. The items on Britain's balance of payments will be of exactly the same kind as those which we studied in the previous chapter. First, there will be the imports and exports of 'visible' and 'invisible' goods and services. The value of exports will represent a receipt in Britain's 'Balance of Payments'. It will show the value, in pounds sterling, of the foreign currency paid to Britain for her 'visible' and 'invisible' exports during the year. In our 'two-country world' the whole of this foreign currency received will, of course, be dollars. In the real world it will be an amount made up of all kinds of currencies. The counterpart of these receipts from exports will be the payments made by Britain for 'visible' and 'invisible' imports.

These two items, receipts earned by British exports and payments made to those who supply Britain's imports, will make up the 'Balance of Trade'. Britain's payments for 'visible' and 'invisible' imports normally exceed her receipts from her exports, so that there is a 'deficit' on the balance of trade. In other words, Britain's 'current trading account'—the receipts and payments resulting from 'current trading'—usually shows a debit balance. This deficit on current account has to be made up on capital account, for, like all accounts, the balance of payments as a whole must balance. Not all countries will have debit balances on their current trading accounts; some will have balance of trade surpluses. Indeed, on our simplifying assumption that there are only two countries in the 'world', the current trading deficit on Britain's balance of trade will merely be the mirror image of a *surplus* on America's current trading account.

The remainder of Britain's foreign exchange transactions must now be introduced, in order to turn the 'Balance of Trade' into the balance of payments. These transactions will all represent capital movements. The most important items will be long-term and short-term investment. Where Britain lends money to foreigners by buying either short- or long-term overseas investments, the money spent will represent a 'payment out' in Britain's balance of payments. Similarly, any money which foreigners lend *to* Britain will be entered in the receipts side of Britain's foreign payments account. Two further items remain. First, there may be some receipts by Britain because people wish to 'hoard' sterling; there may be 'payments out' if people prefer to 'hoard' dollars. Second, there will be payments made by the British Government to foreigners, and receipts by the British Government from foreigners. When all these payments on both current and capital account have been added together, and all the receipts too, there may be either a surplus of receipts over payments—a balance of payments surplus. Alternatively, if total payments exceed total receipts there will be a balance of payments deficit—a deficit on all Britain's transactions, current and capital, with the rest of the world. In our 'two-country' world, a surplus on Britain's balance of payments will be matched by an identical deficit on America's balance of payments; the British deficit on foreign account will be the mirror image of an identical American surplus.

For, in the world as a whole, deficits and surpluses must exactly cancel out. No country can have a deficit without being a debtor to some other country; and the debts of the borrowers will obviously always equal the loans of the lenders. This raises a further point. We have already said that the balance of payments, like any double-entry book-keeping account, *must* balance. How, then, do we come to say that Britain can have either a surplus or a deficit on the balance of payments ? The answer is that whilst the balance of payments always *must* balance, the process by which that balance is brought about will differ—and may indeed be quite painful where there is a large deficit.

Let us suppose that Britain, as happened in several immediate post-war years, has a deficit on her balance of payments—the now familiar 'dollar gap'. In our simple 'world', this implies that the United States has a surplus on her balance of payments which just equals Britain's deficit. The British balance of payments must balance in one way or another, as indeed must the American. Therefore, the deficit on her trading and investment account, increased or decreased as the case may be by the movement of hoards of 'hot' money, must be exactly offset in one way or another. At the current foreign exchange rate the dollar gap may be filled by running down Britain's gold and other foreign exchange reserves ; by a gift or loan (in dollars) from the American Government, or by the imposition of exchange control to reduce Britain's purchases of foreign currency. If these three policies, individually or together, are not sufficient, the only alternatives are either devaluation or deflation.

Let us consider these three possible ways of filling the 'dollar gap'. Governments will not normally wish to allow the foreign exchange value of their currency to fall. This is a question, as much as anything, of political and economic prestige. The first reaction to the emergence of a balance of payments deficit in a country will almost always be to allow that particular country's gold and foreign exchange reserves to fall. Gold is important in this context because, up to the present at least, it represents a kind of 'money' which all countries will accept gladly. Similarly, a country will normally accept its own currency in payment for a debt. Britain can therefore close its 'dollar gap', for a short period of time, by itself providing dollars with which British importers can pay off their debts to America. In the early stages, this will happen automatically. The Exchange Equalisation Fund will wish to maintain the foreign exchange value of the pound, which will have begun to 'sag' when the British supply of pounds in exchange for dollars begins to exceed the demand for them. It will therefore use the British foreign exchange reserves to supply dollars on the foreign exchange market, and to buying up pounds.

Such a policy cannot, however, go on for ever. The Exchange Equalisation Fund will clearly be able to deal in this way with purely seasonal deficits or with other short-lived dollar shortages. But any large, or long-term, deficit will soon reduce the country's foreign exchange reserves so seriously that other methods of 'closing the dollar gap' will have to be used.

The simplest, of course, is to increase the supply of dollars available to Britain by persuading the American Government to make either a gift or a loan to Britain, as happened at the end of the Second World War. But even such a loan is, of course, no long-term solution. It can only be looked on legitimately as a temporary way of easing the immediate foreign exchange problem until more radical solutions to it, for example, an 'export drive', can be put into operation.

If, as is extremely likely, other countries are unwilling to lend money to a Britain which is not strong enough to finance her own foreign trade, a likely solution would be exchange control. Britain instituted such a system when war broke out in 1939, and it has been used since 1945 as a major way of preventing the emergence of an impossibly large dollar deficit. The main feature of such a policy will be strict controls over the amount of foreign currency which can be spent on imports— and hence over the imports themselves. It is also likely that such exchange control will mean discrimination against some currencies. For example, if dollars are short but lire are not, British importers will be given much more generous treatment when they wish to buy goods from Italy than when they want to import from the U.S.A. To be successful, exchange control must cover *all* transactions. For example, the British exchange control system since 1945 has kept an extremely close check on the size of foreign travel allowances. British people going on holiday to Europe have only been allowed to spend relatively small amounts of money. Britons going on a post-war holiday to America have not been allowed, up to the time of writing, to spend any dollars at all. There has been even tighter control over the amount of *pound notes* which British tourists could take abroad, for these can easily be sold abroad surreptitiously for foreign currency, thereby worsening the balance of payments position.

There has also been control over the 'export of capital' from Britain; the supply of sterling on the foreign exchange market has been kept down by strict control, not only over trade and foreign travel, but also by ensuring that large amounts of capital were not transferred from Britain to, say, America. Control over capital movements has represented an important weapon for preventing sudden and large changes in the sterling foreign exchange rate, and also in the size of any post-war British balance of payments deficit. As we have seen earlier, it is capital movements which are likely to cause the biggest and most unexpected inflows and outflows of any currency.

It should perhaps be noted that where exchange control is used as a way of restricting imports, it will usually imply the need also for fixing import quotas for various types of product. Only in this way will the exchange control authorities be able easily to keep track of what is going on. Similarly, exchange control may be supplemented by tariffs on imports. All these weapons, exchange control, quotas, tariffs, suffer from the same fundamental objection. By keeping out foreign imports, they bolster up inefficiency in domestic industries, and they do so at the expense of the home consumer.

The kinds of foreign exchange policy which we have so far considered have been those which will be used in an attempt to preserve the exchange value of a currency and which also allow full employment to be maintained. The 'traditional' solution to a balance of payments deficit, that is to say the one used until the depression of the 1930's and its aftermath caused a 'revolution' in economic thinking, was to raise rates of interest. In the short period this led to an influx of short-term funds from other countries and provided a temporary palliative. In the long run, high rates of interest at home reduced investment and lowered the levels of both domestic income and prices. The result was to cause an automatic fall in imports and, if prices of goods for export fell far enough, a rise in exports. The desirability of such a policy is now questioned.

In the first place, it almost certainly means abandoning full employment, and at present full employment seems to be more important than maintaining the foreign exchange rate, which is after all largely a question of mere national pride. Second, it is unlikely that a really serious balance of payments deficit could be cured without deliberately reducing the level of wages as well as increasing the rate of interest. It was as a result of such an attempt to lower wages in the 1920's that British opinion finally turned against deflation as a cure for a balance of payments deficit.

The older tradition, which says 'when in deficit deflate', has therefore been replaced by a newer one which says, 'when in deficit devalue'. If Britain cannot fill her dollar gap by borrowing or by exchange control, and if she is unwilling to undergo the social problems of deflation and unemployment, there is only one solution—the foreign exchange value of the pound must fall. This is, of course, what would happen on a free foreign exchange market. A dollar gap merely means that the demand of Americans for pounds on the foreign exchange market has fallen short of the British supply of pounds in exchange for dollars. The automatic result, with a completely free foreign exchange market, would be for the pound to 'depreciate'; its price in terms of dollars would fall. At present, however, it is not thought desirable to allow completely free foreign exchange rates. There are obvious advantages to traders if Governments undertake to keep exchange rates stable over considerable periods of time; and this, of course, is the aim of the Exchange Equalisation Fund, as indeed, it was an automatic result of the pre-1914 Gold Standard. The British Government therefore nowadays sets an 'official' exchange rate for sterling, and this rate is only changed discontinuously. Such a change will come when the rate of exchange is so badly out of line with what seems most satisfactory that a considerable change is needed. Thus, if a dollar deficit has lasted for some time and there is no other way of dealing with it, the British Government will 'devalue' the pound. In 1949, for example, 'devaluation' lowered the price of one pound from $4.03 to $2.80. The distinction between a 'depreciation' in the value of a currency and 'devaluation' is that the former results from the workings of the market; the latter represents the result of a deliberate decision by the Government.

The results of devaluation will usually be to improve a country's balance of payments. First, capital movements will become favourable. The likelihood of devaluation is usually noticed by the market some time before it actually happens. There will, therefore, usually be a 'run' on the currency in question as holders of 'hot money' buy other currencies in order to repurchase the suspect currency, when devaluation has actually occurred. Once devaluation is an accomplished fact, such 'hot money' is likely to return, and this return will strengthen the value of the devalued currency. Second, there will be effects on the volume of the devaluing country's exports and imports. Devaluation is only likely to occur where the prices of a country's exports are 'too high' compared with prices in the rest of the world, perhaps because of inflation within the country. Devaluation will, at any rate temporarily, improve the devaluing country's trading position.

Returning to our example from the previous chapter, let us suppose that an American car sells for $1200. If the rate of exchange is £1 = $4, then a Briton who wants to import an American car will have to pay £300 for it. If the pound is now 'devalued' so that the rate of exchange becomes £1 = $3, American export prices will rise in terms of sterling. The American car will now cost £400 instead of £300. At the same time, the dollar prices of British exports will fall. For example, a selection of British woollen goods worth £400 would cost $1600 in America before devaluation. After devaluation, they would cost only $1200.

The result of a devaluation of the pound is therefore to lower the prices, in terms of their own currencies, which foreigners have to pay for British exports, and to raise the prices (in pounds sterling) which have to be paid in Britain for foreign goods. In any normal situation this will automatically reduce the volume of imports into Britain. The higher sterling prices of imports will cause people to buy less of them. Similarly, the lower prices, in terms of foreign currencies, of British exports will enable them to be sold more easily in foreign countries.

Provided the foreign demand for British exports and the British home demand for foreign imports are moderately elastic, devaluation will markedly improve the balance of payments position. This can be shown quite easily.

Let us consider our two countries—the U.S.A. and Great Britain. If the American demand for British goods is elastic, it follows that the fall in the dollar prices of British goods caused by devaluation will lead to an increased total dollar expenditure on them. For example, let us suppose that, before devaluation, with the rate of exchange at £1 = $4, American consumers spent $8 million on British goods—that is to say, £2 million at the pre-devaluation exchange rate. If the exchange rate is now lowered, by devaluation, to £1 = $3, the elastic demand in the U.S.A. for British goods will lead to an increase in dollar expenditure on them, say from $8 million to $12 million. At the new, devalued rate of exchange this will mean a sterling expenditure of £4 million.

Devaluation will therefore raise the total sterling receipts of

British exporters from £2 million to £4 million. If the British demand for foreign goods is also elastic, devaluation will mean that Britain spends a smaller total amount of sterling on its imports. As always, a rise in the price of goods with an elastic demand will lower total expenditure on them. Thus, where the foreign demand for British exports is elastic, the total amount of sterling received from foreigners in payment for British goods will increase; on the other hand, Britain's sterling expenditure on foreign goods will also diminish, provided only that British demand for foreign goods is also elastic. These increased sterling receipts and reduced sterling payments will considerably improve the British balance of payments.

It follows from the above example, however, that it is not even necessary for these two demands to be elastic in the strict sense of the term for the balance of payments position to be improved by devaluation. Even if the American demand for British goods is inelastic in the strict sense, so that the total amount of *dollars* spent on them falls, the total amount of sterling received in Britain cannot possibly fall. For example, even if devaluation of the sterling exchange rate from £1 = $4 to £1 = $3 reduces American expenditure on British goods from $8 million to $6 million, Britain's total *sterling* receipts will remain unaltered at £2 million. And this result can only occur if the total physical quantity of British goods bought remains *completely unchanged* when their price falls—a most unlikely case. The total amount of *sterling* received from British exports is almost certain to rise after devaluation. The balance of payments can therefore improve, even if the British demand for imports is inelastic and a rise in their price leads to an increased total sterling outlay on them. It can do so provided only that the increase in sterling receipts from exports is greater than the increase in sterling expenditure on imports. These are not very stringent conditions.

One can therefore conclude that, even if the foreign demand for British exports and the British demand for foreign goods are inelastic in the strict sense, this need not matter. Only if *both* of these demands are extremely inelastic is devaluation likely to lead to a worsening of the balance of payments position. For only in this case will there be a considerable increase in Britain's sterling payments for imports which is not offset by the rise in the sterling receipts from American expenditure on British goods. And it is only in these latter circumstances that devaluation would actively *worsen* a British balance of payments deficit.

L

But even where, as is likely, these vital elasticities of demand are high enough to improve the devaluing country's balance of payments position, it does not follow that devaluation will represent a final solution to its problems. The increase in exports can only occur if British export industries are able to expand their output readily. If there is unemployment in Britain, this may be simple. But if there is full employment, some way will have to be found, perhaps by increasing the size of the budget surplus, to reduce aggregate expenditure within Britain and so free productive resources which can be used to increase the volume of exports. Again, especially in a country like Britain, the prices paid by wage earners who are spending their incomes will depend to a substantial extent on import prices. Devaluation will therefore not only raise import prices, it will increase the British worker's 'cost of living'. As a result, there is likely to be pressure for wage increases. This in its turn will raise the price of British exports and lower their volume. So, especially where there is full employment in a country, there is a danger that devaluation will be self-defeating. It will merely bring a short-lived respite to the balance of payments until rising import prices lead to higher wages, higher export prices, fewer exports, and a return of the balance of payments deficit.

This leads us to two important questions. Does a full employment policy always mean that a country will have a deficit on its balance of payments? And, if so, is the only remedy a progressive devaluation of the country's currency?

It is generally agreed that the fact that a country has to carry out its full employment policy in a world economy, where all countries independently pursue their own policies, will lead to two major difficulties. First, the multiplier will not work in quite the way we showed in Chapter IX. We saw there that the size of the multiplier depends on the proportion of their incomes which people save. High savings mean that a given volume of Government spending raises income less substantially than where little is saved. But in a world economy, the existence of foreign trade will also reduce the size of the multiplier within a country. For the 'multiplier effects' of any consumption expenditure on imports will be felt in the country which supplies the imports, and not in the country which engages in 'public works' expenditure in an effort to increase its own employment. In a country with much foreign trade, such 'leakages' are likely to be quite significant.

It follows that a single country may well run into problems if it attempts to maintain full employment when other countries are depressed, these problems being less serious the less important is international trade in that country's economy. First, there is the likelihood that some of the multiplier effects of any Government investment programme will be felt in other countries. This will increase the amount of money that the Government has to spend on investment in order to obtain a given rise in the national income. Where the 'leakages' through foreign trade are very large, there may be the added difficulty that Governments will object to spending money merely to increase the level of employment in countries which are too indolent to pursue a full employment policy of their own.

A second difficulty facing a country that attempts to maintain full employment in a world of depression is this. The higher the level of economic activity in any country is, the greater will be its demand for imports. In a depressed world, then, a country pursuing a full employment policy is unlikely to be able to pay for all these imports with its own exports. Depressed foreign countries will not be able to afford to buy such exports. Indeed, part of the country's full employment policy may be to sell motor-cars, that were previously exported, on the home market. The fully employed country's demand for imports may therefore be so large that these imports cannot be paid for by exports or loans from abroad; a full employment policy may consequently mean a balance of payments deficit.

We can now answer the two questions posed earlier. First, the pursuit of a full employment policy is almost certain to mean a deficit on the balance of payments *unless* many countries in the world are simultaneously trying to sustain employment. Even if all other countries *are* pursuing full employment policies, however, any given country may run into trouble if its own full employment policy means that its internal prices are rising more quickly than are prices in other countries. For this, again, may reduce exports and increase imports. It is generally agreed that unless there is an actual or tacit agreement among all countries to try to achieve full employment all the time, it is only a relatively small country, with little international trade, which is likely to be able to preserve its level of employment without experiencing a deficit on its balance of payments.

Second, if the pursuit of a full employment policy does lead to balance of payments deficits, devaluation may well be the only way out. Only by deliberately reducing its export prices through a devaluation, which will simultaneously make imports dearer, may a country be able to improve its balance of payments position. But this is a desperate remedy. We have already seen that devaluation is likely to lead to wage increases that in time will destroy the benefits which devaluation gives; and the process may become progressive. Worse than that, there is a real danger that countries which engage in devaluation will be accused of trying to 'export their unemployment'. The reaction may well be 'competitive devaluation' by other countries, and perhaps the building of tariff barriers against the devaluing countries. Bitter experience of such 'beggar-my-neighbour' policies in the 1930's has led the post-war world to try to avoid them. Here, more than ever, international co-operation is needed; to see that a country's desire for full employment does not lead to competitive devaluation.

One of the aims of the International Monetary Fund is to prevent this kind of policy being pursued in the post-war world. Members of the Fund promise to refrain from competitive devaluation. In addition, the Fund holds large amounts of the various currencies of the world. Instead of having to devalue whenever a balance of payments deficit emerges, countries can borrow foreign currency from the International Monetary Fund, thereby obtaining a 'breathing space' during which they can try to solve their problems without resort to devaluation.

Economists today seem agreed that in the absence of international co-operation to maintain full employment and to prevent competitive devaluation, it may often be extremely difficult for any country to maintain both full employment *and* a stable foreign exchange rate. This is why we have passed from the older tradition which met a balance of payments deficit by deflation to the newer tradition which turns, albeit as a last resort, to devaluation.

More recently, yet a third tradition seems to be growing up. This asks whether the chronic 'softness' of sterling—the chronic 'hardness' of the dollar—may not both reflect a fundamental lack of equilibrium in the world economy. Maybe, the argument runs, the time is now past when the nations of Western Europe could base their economies on the export of manufactured goods that were made from cheap, imported raw materials. Perhaps the 'terms of trade' have turned against Western Europe so that they will never again be able to obtain the same volume of imports by supplying a given volume of exports. Whether or not this is a correct argument, it is certainly true that the 'terms of trade' have deteriorated seriously for the world's manufacturing nations since the 1930's.

It should not, of course, be supposed that it is only such long-term changes in the terms of trade that are important. Short-term changes can be quite crucial. For example, while the post-Korean war boom raised the prices of Britain's imported raw materials very substantially, it did not cause a rise in the prices of her own manufactured export goods that was at all comparable. A given volume of British exports therefore bought a significantly smaller volume of imported raw materials— Britain's 'terms of trade' deteriorated. This was one reason for the 'sterling crisis' of 1951. Britain, in 1951, had to pay very much more for her imports; yet her receipts from a more or less given volume of exports increased very little. Thus the balance of payments position worsened.

In the same way, an improvement in Britain's terms of trade after the end of 1951 did much to help the recovery of sterling that took place after the return to power of the Conservative Government in 1951. Import prices fell more than export prices; and the same volume of imports could therefore be paid for with fewer exports—the 'terms of trade' had improved.

One final point remains. The reader will have noticed that we have slipped quite easily from discussing a 'two-country' world to discussing the problems of the world as it really is. This fact in itself shows how little the basic problems of international trade alter when one turns from the relations between only two countries to the relations between many. There will, however, be some difficulties. Although, on the face of it, a balance of payments surplus seems to be the same thing whether it is a surplus of francs, marks or dollars, this may not be so. In a world where one cannot easily convert one currency into another, a surplus with one country may not be available to offset a deficit with another. For example, where the United States has earned pounds by showing films in Britain, this sterling has not been available to pay off United States debts to, say, Switzerland. Much of it has not even been repayable to America in dollars. The British Government has insisted on keeping much of these earnings from films in Britain.

It follows that the post-war world is one where 'multilateral' trade has been difficult to carry out. 'Blocked' accounts and

L 2

the like have meant that countries have often had to 'balance their trade' exactly with each of the other countries. 'Bilateral' trade, where earnings from one country cannot be used to pay for goods from others, has become all too common.

It is for this reason that the early 1950's have been years when the 'convertibility' of one currency into another has been a widespread goal. For where currencies are 'convertible', countries find it immeasurably easier to trade. There is no need for 'bilateral', exactly balanced, trade. All currencies can be changed into all other currencies. Hence a 'multilateral' system, where a British export of machinery to Africa can yield earnings that can be used to finance the import of cotton from America, would again become a reality, to the benefit of all concerned.

CHAPTER XIV

ECONOMIC POLICY

In their professional, as distinct from their private, life, economists are rarely dogmatic about the kind of economic policy which 'ought' to be followed in a country. Certainly no economist has the right to feel that his particular professional knowledge gives him the right to lay down the law about the most desirable economic policies. A knowledge of economics cannot make a man's mind up for him; it can only help him to make his mind up for himself, by showing up the flaws in the assumptions and the logical reasoning of any argument that he may put forward. The basic reason for this somewhat surprising modesty on the part of economists is that to make policy prescriptions inevitably means making 'value judgments'. It means producing recommendations that cannot be justified by pure scientific analysis but depend on one's own feelings and views.

It is important that economists should always make it quite clear that their policy recommendations are in no way 'scientific'. For the ordinary man, who knows that economics is a specialised science, may well be led into thinking that a particular recommendation is 'scientific' merely because it is expressed in the economist's special jargon. Perhaps even more important is the danger that the economist himself may produce confused results if he tries to combine economic analysis with political propaganda. It is always so much easier to reach the conclusion one wants to reach rather than the conclusion one *ought* to reach. This is particularly so if one has a strong preconceived idea, based on one's political views, of the result one would like to achieve.

We have not been able to live up to such high ideals in this book. We have erred to the extent of smuggling in a few value judgments about which the opinion of modern economists is strongly agreed. For example, we have adopted the common view that a monopoly which earns high profits and charges high prices is 'wrong'. Similarly, we have implied that mass unemployment is 'bad', and a deliberate policy of curing unemployment by a budget deficit is 'good'.

In this chapter we shall try to show the kind of policies which present-day economists prescribe, and how far these policies can be justified on a strictly scientific basis. First, we must discuss the criterion by which economists class economic policies as 'good' or 'bad'. This criterion is simple. Economists usually assume that a policy is 'good' if it helps to increase the 'economic welfare' of the community. By economic welfare, or well-being, they mean the satisfaction which the community derives from consuming goods and services. It follows that the 'best' economic policy will be that which 'maximises economic welfare'. In other words, the 'best' policy is that which gives the greatest possible satisfaction to the community through the consumption of goods and services.

Economists therefore make their policy recommendations on the assumption that the main concern of any Government is to 'maximise' satisfactions in its own country by using its 'scarce resources' to the best possible advantage. There will be qualifications to this aim, because such a simple goal cannot be the only end of a modern community. Such qualifications will emerge as we proceed.

Let us begin by discussing a problem which can be solved on the basis of this simple assumption that the Government wishes merely to 'maximise economic welfare'. We have already seen that in modern economies there is much redistribution of income through progressive taxation, because it is generally felt that greater equality of incomes than would otherwise exist is desirable. This view is based, first, on the desirability of mitigating want as such, and, second, on the need to abolish extremes of wealth and poverty and so eliminate class distinctions based on the possession of very high incomes. We shall now show the way in which economists can justify contentions about the most desirable distribution of income in a society.

Let us begin by hunting for a reasonable hypothesis on which to base the analysis. There are various views which one can take. First, there are many people who sincerely believe that an equal distribution income is either unequivocally good or unequivocally bad. There is no arguing with such an approach. Other people try to avoid making any judgment at all about such a difficult question as what the 'best' distribution of the national income is. They believe in an economics which is entirely free from such absolute judgments. We cannot agree with that view; for one *can* say something about the 'best' income distribution without being 'unscientific'.

We shall base our analysis on three assumptions. The first two are assumptions of fact; the third is a judgment of value. The first assumption of fact is this. If all prices are constant, a rise of, say, £1 in an individual's income will increase his satisfactions. A further increase of £1 in his income will again increase his satisfactions, but it will do so by a smaller amount. In other words, there exists what we may call the 'law of diminishing marginal satisfaction from income'. The richer the man is, the less satisfaction will a given extra amount of money, say £1, give him.

This first assumption, we have said, is a fact and not a value judgment. It is a fact for the following reason. Let us assume that a man has an income of £100. It is only reasonable to suppose that when he spends this £100 he buys those goods which are most desirable to him. He will buy those goods first which he wants most. He wishes to obtain the greatest possible satisfactions from spending his £100; and if the goods he buys were not the most satisfying combination possible, he would not buy them. The goods which he does *not* buy *must* give him less satisfaction than those which he does buy. They clearly do not give greater satisfactions or he would have bought them instead.

There can therefore be no doubt that the second absolute increment in income which any consumer receives gives him less satisfactions than did the previous (equal) increment. Otherwise, he would have bought the second group of goods first. It follows that the satisfactions derived from spending equal increments in income decrease for all of us as we become richer.

The second assumption is also an assumption of fact, though it would be difficult to prove conclusively. Our first assumption has enabled us to see what successive increments of income are worth to any individual; we now need some way of making comparisons between individuals in order to see which people deserve the biggest incomes and which the smallest. What can we say about the capacity of different people to enjoy income? It seems rather rash to maintain that human beings are all completely unlike each other. There must be some similarities between different human beings, otherwise they would never all be called 'human beings'. Indeed, it seems far more reasonable to argue that all human beings are alike than to argue that all are

different.   Our second assumption is therefore that, in their
ability to derive satisfaction from spending their incomes, people
are all very similar.   For we must always remember one thing.
Whilst we may disagree wholeheartedly with the claim that 'all
men are born equal' in their capacity to enjoy spending their
incomes, there is no need to insist that anyone who says that
they are 'all equal' is a lunatic.   More than this, if a rich man
denies that all men are much the same as each other, and claims
instead that the rich are exquisite and the poor intolerable, is he
not just being conceited?   There are also those equally mis-
guided people who seem to believe that the poor are all capable
of leading a good life and that the rich are all wicked and insensi-
tive to true enjoyments.

It is, of course, obvious that all people are *not* completely
identical.   Some people prefer smoking cigarettes to pipe-
smoking;   others prefer eating sweets to eating chocolates.   But
it certainly does not follow that, just because people like different
things, a man cannot derive the same satisfactions from a pound
spent in one way as another man derives from spending a pound
in a different way.   It may be impossible to prove that one man
derives more enjoyment from Mendelssohn's Violin Concerto
than another man obtains from Beethoven's Violin Concerto.   But
there is no reason why, in fact, they should not both be equally
satisfied.

Let us assume for the moment that our second assumption
takes the strict form of saying that all people are *identical*, not in
their particular tastes, but in their capacity to enjoy income.   It
then follows that if one takes £1 from a richer man and gives it
to a poorer man, one has increased the total satisfaction of the
country.   For since we are assuming that all men are identical,
the principle of 'diminishing marginal satisfaction from income'
shows that the richer man values his 'marginal' pound less highly
than the poorer man does.   The process of redistribution of
income should consequently go on until all incomes are exactly
equal.   Only in this way can one 'maximise the satisfactions of
the community'.   For only at this stage will it be impossible to
increase welfare by taking money from those with incomes which
are above average, thereby giving more satisfaction to the new
recipient than the income gave originally to the man from whom
it is now taken away.

If one assumes that all consumers are identical, it follows that
'national satisfaction' will be at a maximum when all incomes

are equal. In fact, of course, such a bald contention is too strong. Our assumption that all people are *identical* was only made temporarily as a strict version of our real assumption, namely, that all people are very similar. If one makes this latter assumption, however, complete equality of incomes is likely to be quite close to the 'best' position. If the State wishes to attain 'maximum welfare', incomes should, apparently, only vary within a very narrow range.

This conclusion depends not only on our second assumption of fact, that all men are mentally similar in their ability to enjoy income, just as they are physically similar. It also depends on a judgment of value, namely, that if people are, in fact, mentally similar they ought all to be treated in a similar fashion—by being given similar incomes. Even if our second assumption of fact is wrong, however, this policy recommendation may still be correct. Even if all men are 'not equal' in their ability to enjoy incomes, it is, nevertheless, still right to treat them as though they are. This is our value judgment.

Our conclusion may be wrong; if it is, it is the task of those who believe in inequality of income to make a better case for inequality. There is a very important point here. If one asked people whether or not they agreed with equality of incomes, one would usually find that equality was popular with the poor and anathema to the rich. On the other hand, if one asked a rich man whether he would still believe in inequality of income, even if it meant that he had to become very poor, one would be unlikely to find him maintaining his position. Self-interest would usually force him to agree that, rather than be a pauper, he would be content to allow greater equality of income. With rich people, the belief in inequality in incomes is not really a belief in inequality *as such*; it is more likely to be based on the realisation that with greater equality of income they would be much worse off.

There is, however, a different and very powerful argument against equality of incomes, especially where this is achieved by means of redistributive taxation. This is the 'incentives' argument. Many modern countries redistribute income from rich to poor by means of a highly progressive tax system; and we have already seen that a progressive income tax will probably reduce incentives to work—especially at high levels of income, where rates of tax are also very high. Some indirect tax systems may also tend to have this effect. There is little objection to high rates of tax on 'luxuries' like jewellery, expensive motor-cars, and so on, which are bought by the rich rather than the poor. But there are strong objections to high taxes on the 'necessities', bread, milk and so on, on which the poor spend a relatively large proportion of their incomes. So the sales taxes paid by people with large incomes will be high; the system will be 'progressive'. And such taxation will also tend to reduce incentives to work. For it makes no difference to the taxpayer whether he pays only an income tax of, say, 50 per cent on the income he receives for working an extra 'marginal' hour, or whether he pays no income tax, but a 100 per cent purchase tax doubles the prices of all the goods that these 'marginal' earnings will buy. Highly progressive income and purchase taxes may well both damage incentives to work. Whichever type of tax is levied, there is a real danger that less work will be done by those people who earn the highest incomes if a sharply progressive tax system is used to redistribute income. Similarly, we have seen that progressive income taxes may discourage the rich from using their savings to help in the financing of real investment in industry.

We have implied, in Chapter X, that perhaps those who bemoan the damaging effects of a highly progressive tax system are being too gloomy. But there is certainly no reason to suppose that incentives to work and save are left completely unchanged by progressive taxes. The whole difficulty of this problem is that few hard facts are known. It is therefore quite possible that, in a world where the only politically acceptable method of redistribution of the national income is through the tax system, the desire to make the distribution of the national income more equal may also mean that the national income itself is smaller than it might have been. In other words, it is quite possible that we can either choose to give the working class a larger share of a national income that is growing only slowly, because incentives are blunted by progressive taxation; or perhaps we can choose to give them a smaller share of a national income that is growing very rapidly, unhampered by any 'disincentive' effects of progressive taxes. As we have said, there is no absolute proof that this really is the choice confronting us. But the 'incentives' argument—that we have the choice between a small share in a larger (and growing) income and a large share in a smaller (and static) income—is certainly a perfectly respectable one.

A further argument against equality of income is that it will reduce the savings of the community. The rich will not be able to save 'out of their superfluity'. Money which would have been saved by a rich man will probably, if incomes are made more equal, be spent by a poorer one. Thus, at times when progress in the economy depends on large savings to finance investment in industry, considerable inequality of income may be desirable. For there are likely to be more savings when incomes are unequal than when they are equal.

The important thing here, however, is to realise that there are two quite independent arguments which economists can put forward about the distribution of income. The first is that an *equal* distribution of a *given* income will 'maximise welfare' at the present. The second is that an *equal* distribution of income may mean that the national income fails to grow as rapidly as it would have done with greater inequality. There is no way of reaching a final judgment without relying almost wholly on one's own opinions and feelings. The really important thing is to realise, as is all too rarely done in current discussions, that there are these two viewpoints from which the problems of income distribution can be approached, and that they tend to lead to different conclusions.

This discussion of the 'best' distribution of income shows how easy disagreement about the results of an economic policy can be. The basic disagreement over economic policy today is, however, a different one. The main issue dividing those interested in current affairs seems to be the choice between planning or socialism (with Communism as an extreme form) and anti-social-ism, or *laissez-faire*. In this dispute, trained economists in Britain are probably divided fairly evenly between the two sides. There is much support among economists for the typically British compromise of the 'mixed' economy, as it exists in Britain today. At present a considerable sector of the British economy lies either under the direct control of the Government itself, or is run by nationalised industries and 'Public Utility' Companies. There is also a very large and important private sector of the economy, where the influence of Government controls is small. In practice, there can at present be no real question in Britain of either 'one hundred per cent' socialism or 'one hundred per cent' *laissez-faire*. The 'mixed' economy is not likely to disappear for many years. In the circumstances, the only practical problem is whether there is a need for a little more or a little less planning, a little more or a little less freedom from Government controls.

There are, moreover, strong arguments against either com-plete socialism or complete *laissez-faire*. The real objection to socialism is that it inevitably breeds the bureaucrat; and he suffers from the important fault, immortalised in the story of the mother who sends her daughter into the garden with the command, 'Go and see what little Johnny is doing; and tell him not to'. The danger that, to the bureaucrat, private industry will automatically seem to behave just as badly as 'little Johnny' is one which raises a strong objection to socialism—and even more so to Communism. Coupled with this fault of the bureaucrat is the rather similar view of many socialists that the State knows better than the individual what is in the individual's best interest. This is an equally undesirable attitude.

There is also a very strong objection to complete *laissez-faire*. The claim that, in a completely unplanned society, all men receive the jobs, the incomes and the status which they deserve is just not true. The 'self-made' man does not succeed solely because of merit; there is always a large element of luck.

The specific contribution of economists to this debate is, on the one hand, to point to the social function of the pricing system and, on the other, to call attention to its defects. The *laissez-faire* case is that the community's scarce resources have to be allocated to the production of goods and services, and that the most rational way of doing this is by allowing individual consumers to spend their incomes as they wish. If much money is spent on a good, much of it will be produced, and vice versa. Production is thus adjusted, by the 'impersonal' working of the pricing system, to accord with changes in consumers' tastes.

On the other hand, an uncontrolled pricing system suffers from three defects. First, it cannot ensure the satisfaction of 'collective wants', such as those discussed at the beginning of Chapter X. Second, some control over the 'natural' monopolies referred to on page 40 is often necessary to prevent the 'exploitation' of the consumer. Left to itself, the pricing system would allow such firms to earn monopoly 'rents' over and above the 'normal' profits needed to keep them in business. Third, whilst consumers obtain satisfactions from consuming goods, they may in so doing simultaneously cause losses of satisfaction to other people. The stock textbook example is where production of a good for consumption by one group of consumers may mean the creation of factory smoke which causes inconvenience to other people. Such intangible losses are difficult to measure precisely but they can be quite significant, and the uncontrolled pricing system takes no account of them.

Another choice which seems to confront most Governments today is that between unemployment and inflation. Pursuing a full employment policy is rather like walking along a tightrope. On one side lies deflation and depression; on the other side lies inflation and rising prices. Unless the Government possesses an as yet undreamed-of ability, it is likely that the task of maintaining full employment without inflation will prove too difficult for it. In practice, the choice is usually between an employment policy that is too weak, and does not completely abolish all unemployment, and a policy that is so strong that it causes some inflation. In these circumstances, the economist is often asked to say which is worse, unemployment or inflation.

Most people are agreed that unemployment is unequivocally bad. The 'Economics of Waste', where men and machines are idle and where all the social problems of unemployment arise, is something that the post-war generations in all countries are determined never to experience.

But what of the alternative—inflation? It is much harder for economists to say anything about this; but they can at least point to a negative conclusion. Once full employment has been reached, one cannot increase standards of living by increasing people's money incomes. These increased incomes will merely be swallowed up in rising prices; and no one will be any better off in real terms. The only way to raise real incomes is to increase the nation's *productivity*. Nevertheless, there seems to be common acceptance of the view that *if* full employment does imply a certain measure of mild inflation, then that inflation is the price which must be paid to avoid the kind of mass unemployment that occurred in the 1930's. Whether inflation will itself lead to equally grave economic and social problems as those arising from mass unemployment, time alone can tell. At present, given the choice, most people in Great Britain seem to prefer inflation to unemployment.

We conclude this chapter by discussing one piece of technical apparatus which economists have developed in an attempt to solve policy problems without needing to make value judgments. Most economic policies cannot be put into operation without benefiting some people at the expense of others. This immediately raises the problem: how can we compare the loss suffered by one person, A, with the gain accruing to another person, B? Such a problem will arise in making all the most interesting practical policy decisions. For example, Governments often have to decide whether to tax Peter in order that Paul's food may be subsidised, his rent reduced, or his children sent to school free. Economists have therefore devised a test by which, given sufficient information, they can show whether the gain to the one person will exceed the loss to the other. This test is known as the 'compensation principle'. The 'compensation principle' says that if a new policy makes A so much better off that he could 'compensate' B for the loss which the policy causes to him, *and yet* still be better off than originally, then the policy would increase 'welfare'. If the gainer cannot so 'compensate' the loser, then the policy would decrease the satisfactions of the community.

The simplest way of looking at the compensation principle is this. Assume that a policy change is made, and that A becomes better off at the expense of B. The State now levies a money tax on A which just cancels out the benefit which he has received; similarly, the Government pays a money grant to B which just cancels out the loss that he suffered by the change in policy. The question now is, will the Government be able to take more money away from A in taxes than it has to pay to B? If so, A has gained more than B has lost. In other words, A would gain so much from the change that he could 'bribe' B not to object to the change and still remain better off than he would have been without the change. The policy change has unequivocally increased 'welfare'.

To put the point more generally, if a policy change makes some people in a country better off and others worse off, has it increased the 'total welfare' of the country? The answer is that it *has* increased welfare if those who have gained from the change can 'bribe' the losers not to reverse the change, and yet these gainers remain better off because of the new policy, even after they have paid the 'bribes'. The compensation principle shows that, in this particular instance, the policy change would benefit the community as a whole.

We can now explain the traditional case for free trade, a case which has always had the support of economists. With the simple kind of assumption that we are using, the position is that the removal of an import duty would be desirable if it left the community as a whole better off. This would be the case where the consumers who benefited from lower prices of imports after the tariff had been removed were able to 'compensate' the industries which suffered a loss of income because of the increase in foreign competition, and yet these consumers remained better off because of the change to free trade. Most economists think that this could happen. Of course, if the gainers *could not* compensate the losers without themselves being worse off than when the tariff was in existence, the change to free trade would not be a change for the better.

Unfortunately, even the compensation principle does not completely remove the need for value judgments. The economist can now say that the import duty should be abolished and compensation paid *if necessary*. But the decision whether to pay that compensation still has to be taken; and it is not a decision which can be made on purely economic grounds. One has to face up to the fact that, in economics, there is hardly ever any clear-cut evidence on the desirability or otherwise of a given policy. The economist can certainly help the politician by explaining, as best he can, the true facts of the situation and the probable results of any change in policy. But the final decision cannot be made by the economist as such. The responsibility for the final decision on any economic policy must always lie with the politician and the citizen.

INDEX